The Amarna Letters

SCRIPTURAL RESEARCH INSTITUTE
Published by Digital Ink Productions, 2021

Copyright

While every precaution has been taken in the preparation of this book, the publisher assumes no responsibility for errors or omissions, or for damages resulting from the use of the information contained herein.

The Amarna Letters

Digital edition. January 6, 2021

Copyright © 2021 Scriptural Research Institute.

ISBN: 978-1739069100

These English translations were created by the Scriptural Research Institute in 2020 and 2021, primarily from the published transliterations of Samuel A. B. Mercer, The Tell El-Amarna Tablets. 2 vols. From 1939, and when possible, high-resolution photographs of the tablets. Additionally, the following translations and commentaries were consulted for comparison: Hugo Winckler's The Tell-el-Amarna Letters (1896), and E. Knudtzon's Die El-Amarna-Tafeln. Vorderasiatische Bibliotek, vol. 2. (1907–1915).

The image used for the cover is 'The Procession of the Bull Apis' by Frederick Arthur Bridgman, painted in 1879.

Table of Contents

Forward 1

EA 1: The Pharaoh complains to the Babylonian King 11

EA 1 Notes 17

EA 2: A Proposal of Marriage 19

EA 3: Marriage, grumblings, a palace opening .. 20

EA 4: Royal deceit and threats 22

EA 2 Notes 25

EA 5: Gifts of Egyptian Furniture for the Babylonian Palace 26

EA 5 Notes 28

EA 6: Burna-Buriash II assumes the Throne of Babylon 29

EA 6 Notes 30

EA 7: A Lesson in Geography 31

EA 7 Notes 35

EA 8: Problems in Canaan 36

EA 8 Notes 38

EA 9: Ancient loyalties, new request 39

Table of Contents

EA 9 Notes..41

EA 10: Egyptian Gold and Carpenters..................42

EA 10 Notes..44

EA 15: Assyria Joins the International Scene.....45

EA 15 Notes..46

EA 19: Love and Gold....................................47

EA 19 Notes..50

EA 23: A Goddess Travels to Egypt.................51

EA 26: To the Queen Mother: Some Missing Gold Statues..53

EA 34: The Pharaoh's Reproach Answered........56

EA 34 Notes..57

EA 35: The Hand of Ammit............................58

EA 35 Notes..60

EA 38: A Brotherly Quarrel............................62

EA 38 Notes..64

EA 39: Duty-Free..65

EA 59: From the Citizens of Tunip..................66

EA 59 Notes..68

EA 75: Political Chaos...................................69

TABLE OF CONTENTS

EA 75 Notes...70

EA 86: Complaint to an Official........................71

EA 86 Notes...73

EA 100: The City of Arqa to the King..................75

EA 100 Notes...77

EA 107: Charioteers, but no horses............................78

EA 107 Notes...80

EA 132: The Hope for Peace..81

EA 132 Notes...83

EA 144: Zimreddi of Sidon to Pharaoh..................85

EA 145: Word on Amurru...87

EA 147: A Hymn to the Pharaoh.............................88

EA 147 Notes...89

EA 149: Neither Water nor Wood............................90

EA 153: Ships on Hold..93

EA 154: Orders carried out..94

EA 156: Aziru in Amurru...95

EA 158: Father and Son..96

EA 161: An Absence Explained..................................98

EA 161 Notes...100

Table of Contents

EA 164: Coming, on condition..................101

EA 170: To Aziru in Egypt........................103

EA 170 Notes...105

EA 189: Etakkama of Kadesh....................109

EA 189 Notes...111

EA 197: Biryawaza's plight.......................112

EA 205: Ready for Marching Orders..........114

EA 205 Notes...115

EA 223: Compliance With Orders.............116

EA 233: Work in Progress........................117

EA 234: An Order for Glass.....................118

EA 234 Notes...119

EA 235: An Order for Glass.....................120

EA 244: Labaya attacking Megiddo...........121

EA 245: Assignment of Guilt....................122

EA 245 Note..123

EA 252: Sparing One's Enemies...............124

EA 254: Neither Rebel nor Delinquent.....125

EA 254 Notes...127

EA 255: No destination too far.................129

TABLE OF CONTENTS

EA 255 Notes 130

EA 256: Oaths and Denials 131

EA 256 Notes 133

EA 265: A gift acknowledge 135

EA 265 Notes 136

EA 269: Malik-El to the King 137

EA 270: Extortion 138

EA 271: The Power of the Habirus 139

EA 271 Notes 140

EA 273: From a Queen-Mother 141

EA 273 Notes 142

EA 274: Another city lost 143

EA 280: Another Labaya 144

EA 282: Alone 145

EA 283: Oh to see the king 146

EA 286: A Throne Granted, Not Inherited 147

EA 286 Notes 150

EA 287: A Very Serious Crime 151

EA 287 Notes 154

EA 288: Benign Neglect 156

TABLE OF CONTENTS

EA 288 Note..159

EA 289: A Reckoning Demanded.........................162

EA 289 Notes..164

EA 290: Three Against One.............................166

EA 290 Notes..167

EA 299: A Plea for Help................................168

EA 303: Careful Listening.............................169

EA 314: A shipment of glass..........................170

EA 314 Note..171

EA 316: Postscript to the royal scribe..................172

EA 321: Listening carefully..........................173

EA 321 Notes..174

EA 323: A Royal Order for Glass....................175

EA 325: Preparations Completed....................176

EA 325: Preparations under way....................177

EA 337: Governor of the City........................178

EA 362: A Commissioner Murdered..................179

EA 363: A joint report on the Beqaa Valley.....181

EA 363 Notes..182

EA 364: Justified War..................................183

Table of Contents

EA 364 Notes 184

EA 365: Furnishing Forced Laborers 185

EA 365 Notes 186

EA 366: A rescue operation 187

EA 366 Notes 188

EA 367: From the Pharaoh to Endaruta 189

EA 368: A consignment of personnel 190

EA 368 Notes 191

EA 369: From the Pharaoh to Malik-El 192

EA 370: Preparations completed 193

Also Available in Print 194

Forward

The Amarna Letters are a collection of clay tablets found in the ruins of El Amarna, Egypt, in the 1880s. The city of El Amarna was built by the Pharaoh Akhenaten, during his religious reforms in the 1340s BC, but was then abandoned after he died and Egypt reverted to worshiping the old gods. These letters provide a unique glimpse into a period of Egyptian history, that the Egyptians themselves attempted to erase. After Akhenaten's heir Tutankhamen died, his successor Ay was only able to hold the throne for a few years before Horemheb seized it, and attempted to reunited the Egyptians by erasing all records of Akhenaten's reforms, which included erasing Akhenaten's name from almost every record in Egypt. By this period, El Amarna appears to have already been mostly abandoned, and therefore Egyptologists were able to reconstruct the strange story of Akhenaten's reign, in the middle of the New Kingdom era.

The Amarna letters were recovered from the royal archives in El Amarna, where they appear to have been archived after having been translated for the royal court. The letters are inscribed

Forward

on clay tablets in Cuneiform, the dominant form of writing in Mesopotamia, Canaan, and the neighboring cultures in Anatolia and Cyprus at the time. The shape of the Cuneiform logograms used are Akkadian, the parent form of the later Neo-Babylonian, Neo-Assyrian, and Ugaritic forms of Cuneiform, however, the language used in the Letters is not pure Akkadian. The Letters are between various members of the Egyptian royal court, and many different cities and nations across the Middle East, including Babylon, Assyria, Mitanni, and Cyprus, and therefore the language within the Letters is not consistent. Within the letters from Canaanite cities, all of which were subject to Egypt at the time, several transliterated names are also used, which appears to be a direct precursor to the later development of Ugaritic Cuneiform by 1200 BC, which was an abjad similar to the Canaanite script that was developed by 1000 BC, however, used Cuneiform logograms instead of alphabet-like letters.

The surviving letters were mostly about trade and diplomacy, however, do include a great deal of information about what was happening in the Middle East at the time. In particular, they

Forward

demonstrate how limited Egypt's actual control of its Canaanite holdings were, where the governors of cities were constantly requesting military help to defend themselves against each other, the marauding Habirus, and the Hittite-backed Amorites in northern Canaan. The Amarna Letters were written during the mid-1330s BC, during the reigns of the Pharaohs Amenhotep III and Akhenaten, although it is not always clear when in their respective reigns the letters were written, or even which pharaoh was on the throne at the time.

Many of the tablets are so broken that reconstructing the text is not possible with any level of certainty, however, many are still mostly legible, even after more than 3300 years. Fortunately, the Mesopotamian form of communication was used in Canaan at the time, as Egyptian papyrus would not have survived to the present. The tablets themselves were intended to be translated once they arrived in Egypt, as indicated by postscripts for the translators, that were added to some of the letters. None of the Egyptian translations have survived to the present, however, they must have once existed, and almost certainly on

Forward

papyrus. The royal archives would have almost certainly been filled with papyrus records at the height of El Amarna, however, they no longer exist today.

The Amarna Letters are set during the era of the Israelite book of Judges, using both the Septuagint's chronology, and the Peshitta's chronology, however, before the era of Joshua in the Masoretic chronology. The Amarna Letters include many references to a group of people known as the Habiru (𒄩𒁉𒊒), invading the land of Canaan, which, in any chronology appear to be related to the Hebrews, but not necessarily the specific Hebrews from the books of Joshua and Judges. In the Hebrew book of Genesis, the Hebrews were identified as the descendants of Eber, who was born circa 2900 BC in the Septuagint's chronology, or circa 2500 BC in the Masoretic chronology, presumably in Ur. He was listed as the 6th generation ancestor of Abraham, meaning he had an entire tribe of descendants by Abraham's time, circa 2100 BC. The Hebrew book of Genesis reports that Abraham's father Terah led his family out of Ur, and resettled in Haran, in northern Syria, which would have been circa

Forward

2100 BC. Abraham and his nephew Lot then traveled down to Egypt, where Abraham and his wife Sarah then swindled the pharaoh, before traveling back up into Canaan, where they fought a series of wars against the indigenous Canaanites. According to the Hebrew book of Genesis the Hebrew patriarchs Isaac and Jacob fought additional wars against, and formed various alliances with, the Canaanites, before migrating into Egypt in the 1800s BC.

To some degree, this matches the historical records regarding the Habirus. The Sumerians recorded the existence of an Aramean tribe of nomads called the Habiru as early as the 1800s BC. Over the following 600 years, hundreds of documents from Egypt, Canaan, Syria, Mesopotamia, and Anatolia record nomadic tribes of Habirus plundering their way across the Middle East. These Habiru were not all Semitic, although the bulk of their names do appear to be, with the majority being West-Semitic, implying they originated in Canaan. The Tikunani Prism from Anatolia, dating from around 1550 BC, lists the names of 438 Habiru soldiers, and the majority of them had Hurrian names, implying the Habiru were intermarrying with the locals. Later, Hittite and Mitanni names also appeared within the name lists of Habiru. If the Habiru were the Hebrews, then the Biblical Hebrews appear to be an Egyptianized group of Habiru, as even their leader, Moses, had an Egyptian name.

There are specific correlations between the Habiru in the Amarna Letters, and the Hebrews of the books of Joshua and Judges, however, these could be coincidental. EA 273 refers to Habiru living in the Ayalon Valley, which is today in the northern Palestinian West Bank. In the Septuagint's book of Joshua, the Hebrews conquered and settled in Ayalon under the leader Joshua circa 1505 BC, and at no point were they recorded as being driven out of the valley, which implies that the Habiru in question, were the Hebrews. There is, nevertheless, the contradiction, in that most references to the Habirus were as invading enemies, yet, most Hebrew names and locations of early Hebrew settlement in Canaan listed in the Book of Joshua, appear to have been loyal to the house of Pharaoh.

There is a reference in EA 256 to a thief named Išuia (𒅖𒌑𒅀), which is virtually the

Forward

same as the Aramaic name Yeshua (ישוע), yet, Mut-Hadad, the author of EA 256, is recommending that the Egyptian Commissioner Yanhamu ask this Joshua if Mut-Hadad didn't help to defend him, implying this thief was employed by the Pharaoh, or at least by the commissioner. This Joshua could not have been the Biblical Joshua, as he either would have already been dead, in the Septuagint's and Peshitta's chronologies, or not born yet, in the Masoretic chronology. If all surviving chronologies are wrong, then this could have been the person that the various Books of Joshua were based on, however, there is little linking the thief to the Biblical figure other than his name.

In EA 86, Governor Rib-Hadda of Byblos, requests that the Egyptian official Amenappa order the land of Yarimuta send him grain, because, even though Commissioner Yanhamu claimed he had sent Byblos grain, they had not received it. The Yarimuta in question, is accepted as the same Mount Yarmuta recorded in the stele of Seti I from circa 1280 BC, which was reported as being a Habiru stronghold. This location is also accepted as being the land of Yarmut (יְרְמֹות /

FORWARD

Ιεριμουθ) from the book of Joshua, which had been conquered circa 1505 BC in the Septuagint's chronology, suggesting that the Habiru at Yarimuta, who had sent grain to Byblos, were the Hebrews.

Another Hebrew name that appears in the Amarna Letters was Judah, Iidiia (𒅕𒁺𒅀), which is virtually identical to the Canaanite pronunciation of the name Yhdh (𐤉𐤄𐤃𐤄), and similar to the Neo-Assyrian Cuneiform spelling of Iaudaaa (𒅀𒌑𒁕𒀀𒀀) around 700 years later. This particular Judah, was the author of EA 321, and the governor of Ashkelon, which would later be resettled by the Sea Peoples during the collapse of the New Kingdom in the 1200s BC. The Egyptians called the settlers in the regions the Pelest, and the Hebrews called them the Philistines. This reference to Governor Judah, which precedes the arrival of the Sea Peoples, implies that Hebrews lived in the region at the time. According to the Book of Judges, after Joshua died, the tribe of Judah broke off from the other tribes and migrated south, into what is today central Israel and the southern Palestinian West Bank. This Judahite invasion would have happened sometime after 1480 BC, in the Septuagint's chronology, or the 1200s BC in the Masoretic chronology. EA 321 suggests they also occupied the coastal region before the arrival of the Sea Peoples in the 1200s BC, which supports the chronology of the Septuagint and Peshitta over the Masoretic Texts.

The name Job is also found in the Amarna Letters, as A'iaab (⇔⊨╢⊨◁), which is identical to the Hebrew Iyyov (אִיּוֹב), and Arabic Ayyub (أيوب). The common English pronunciation of 'Job' is derived from the Greek Iob ('Ιώβ), and is used in this English translation as it is the common English form. Someone named Job is mentioned twice in the Amarna Letters, and both are likely the same person. One is the governor of the town of Ashtartu in southern modern Syria, while the other was referred to as helping the Habirus. This Job, was most likely not the Biblical Job or Quranic Ayyub, as that Job would have lived around 2000 BC, based both on the astronomical alignments within the Book of Job and the Testament of Job, as well as the lost Syriac book of Job's reference to Abraham being a close relative of Job. Nevertheless, the name Job appears to have been

Forward

common by the 1300s BC, like the other Hebrew names found in the Amarna Letters.

While a number of the Amarna Letters are too damaged for reconstructions to be included in this collection, a large number are preserved well enough to be translated. This translation uses the modern names of cities and nations when they are known. The transliterated Cuneiform terms are listed in the notes, along with discussions of debated terms.

EA 1: The Pharaoh complains to the Babylonian King

Tell King Kardasman-Enlil of Babylonia,[1] my brother:

A message from the Great King Amenhotep III,[2] of the land of Egypt, your brother.

All is well with me. May all be well with you, your house, your wives, your sons, your officials, your chariotry. May all be exceedingly well across your lands.

All is well with me, and with my house, my wives, my senior officials, my horses, my chariotry, my infantry. Across my lands, it is all very well."

Now I have heard the message you sent to me "You wanted my daughter for your wife, and my sister who my father gave to you is there with you, but now, no one has seen her now and known whether she is alive whether she is dead."

This is what you sent me, on your tablet. These are your words. When have you sent your dignitary who knows your sister? Who can speak with her and identify her and let him speak with her?

EA 1: The Pharaoh complains to the Babylonian King

The men who you sent me were unimportant. One was a man of Sakhar,[3] the other was a donkey-herder of the land of [...damaged text...]. There was not one among them who was close to your father and would know her.

Moreover, as for the envoys that returned to you and said she is not your sister, there was none among the two who knew her, and could tell you, moreover, she is well and alive. Was there given anything into his hand to deliver to her mother?

As for your writing, "You spoke to my envoys while your wives were present, standing before you, saying 'See your mistress who is standing before you' yet my envoys did not recognize her, was it my sister who looks like her? Then you wrote, "My envoys did not recognize her," and you say, "So who has identified her?"

Why don't you send your emissary who will tell you the truth, about the well-being of your sister who is here? Then you can trust the one who enters in to see her house, and the relationship with the king.

EA 1: THE PHARAOH COMPLAINS TO THE BABYLONIAN KING

When you wrote, "Perhaps it was the daughter of some lowly person, either one of the Kaskians[4] or a daughter of the land of Mitanni,[5] or perhaps of the land of Ugarit[6] which my envoys saw. Who can trust those that she is like her? This one did not open her mouth. One can not trust them in anything."

These are your words. And if your sister is dead then why would they conceal her death and why would we present another? Surely the great god Amen knows your sister is alive!

I have appointed her sister to the queen-mother as the mistress of the house [...damaged text...] one bride of [...damaged text...].

[...damaged text...] concerning all of my wives [...damaged text...] which the kings of the land of Egypt [...damaged text...] in the land of Egypt. As you wrote, "As for my daughters who are married to kings they are neighbors, if my envoys go there, they converse with me and they send me a present. The one that is so [...damaged text...]"

EA 1: The Pharaoh complains to the Babylonian King

These are your words. Perhaps the kings who are your neighbors are rich and mighty, and your daughters acquire something from them and they send it to you, but what does she have, your sister who is with me? As soon as she acquires something, then she will send it to you. Is it fitting that you give your daughters in order to acquire a garment from your neighbors?

As for you quoting the words of my father, stop it! Don't speak his words! Moreover, "Establish friendly brotherhood between us."

This is what you wrote, and these are your words. Now, we are brothers, I and you, both of us, but I got angry concerning your envoys because they speak to you, saying, "Nothing is given to us who go to Egypt."

Those who come to me, does one of the two go without taking silver, gold, oil, garments, everything nice more than from another country? Yet he tells lies to the one who sends him! The first time your envoy went off to your father and their mouths spoke lies. The second time they went out and they are telling lies to you.

EA 1: The Pharaoh complains to the Babylonian King

So I said to myself, "If I give them something or if I don't give them, they will tell lies anyway," so I made up my mind about them, and I did not give them more.

As you wrote, "You said to my envoys, 'Your master has no infantry, and the girl he gave to me is not beautiful!'"

These are your words. Not so! Your envoys are speaking lies to you in this manner! If there are warriors or if there aren't, it is known to me. Why is it necessary to ask him if you have infantry or if you have horses? No! Don't listen to your two envoys that you send here in whose mouths are lies! Perhaps they are afraid of you, and so they tell you lies to escape your punishment?

As you said, "He placed my chariots among the chariots of the city rulers, you did not review them separately! You humiliated them before the throng which is there and you did not review them separately."

EA 1: The Pharaoh complains to the Babylonian King

I verify, the chariots are here. I verify, the horses from my country are here! All the chariot horses had to be supplied.

When you sent to my hand a vessel to anoint the head of the girl, you sent to me one gift of pure oil. Are we to laugh?

EA 1 Notes

1 Cuneiform: Karaduniaš (𒃰𒁺𒉌𒼊𒀸)

Karaduniash was the Kassite name for Babylon.

2 Cuneiform: Nibmuaria (𒉆𒈬𒀀𒊑𒅀)

Amenhotep III is accepted by Egyptologists, to have been referred to several ways in the Amarna Texts, including Nibmuaria, Nimuwareya, and Mimmureya, based on his Egyptian prenomen neb Maat Ra (𓎟𓐙𓇳).

3 Cuneiform: Zakara (𒍝𒀀𒊏)

This is believed to be the Sakhar region in Babylonia, which was an animal pasture region at the time.

4 Cuneiform: Kàšká (𒀗𒃻)

The Kaskians were a tribe in Eastern Pontic Anatolia, known from Hittite records. Their name is likely the source of the name of the Caucasus Mountains, where they appear to have been pushed as the Neo-Hittite Empire pushed into their territory in the early 1st-millennium BC. They may be the ancestors of the modern Caucasian ethno-linguistic group, including the Georgians, Abkaz, and Chechens, although that has not been proven conclusively.

EA 1 NOTES

5 Cuneiform: Hanigalbat (𒄩𒉌𒃲𒁁)

Hanigalbat was one of the Cuneiform names believed to refer to the Mitanni civilization, that dominated northern Syria and northern Iraq in the 1300s BC.

6 Cuneiform: Ugarta (𒌷𒌑𒂵𒅈𒋫)

Ugarit (𐎜𐎂𐎗𐎚) was a major Canaanite city on the Mediterranean coast of Syria in the 1300s BC. It was burned to the ground circa 1190 BC by the Sea Peoples.

EA 2: A Proposal of Marriage

Tell King Amenhotep III of Egypt, my brother:

A message from King Kadashman-Enlil of Babylonia.

In my country, all goes well for me. May all be very well for you, your wives, your sons, your officials, your cavalry, your chariotry, and your entire country.

In regards to my brother's writing to me about marriage, saying, "I desire your daughter," why should you not marry her? My daughters are available, but their husbands must be a king or of royal blood. These are the only ones I accept for my daughters. No king has ever given his daughters to anyone who wasn't of royal blood.

[...damaged text...] Your daughters are available, why have you not given me one?

[...damaged text...] fine horses [...damaged text...] 20 wooden [...damaged text...] of gold [...damaged text...] 120 shekels [...damaged text...] I send to you as your greeting gift. 60 shekels of lapis-lazuli I send as the greeting gift of your sister, [...damaged text...] my wife.

EA 3: Marriage, grumblings, a palace opening

Tell King Amenhotep III Of Egypt, my brother:

A message from King Kadashman-Enlil of Babylonia, your brother.

For me, all goes very well. For you, for your household, your wives, and your sons, your country, your chariotry, your cavalry, your officials may all go very well.

In regards to the girl, my daughter, about who you wrote to me regarding marriage, she has become a woman, and she is nubile. Send a delegation to fetch her. Previously my father would send a messenger to you and you did not detain him for very long. You quickly sent him off, and you would also send to my father here a beautiful greeting gift. But now when I sent a messenger to you you have detained him for six years and you have only sent me as my greeting gift in six years 30 minas of gold that looked like silver. That gold was melted down in the presence of Kasi your messenger, and he was a witness. When you celebrated a great festival you did not send

EA 3: Marriage, Grumblings, a Palace Opening

your messenger to me saying "Come to eat and drink."

Nor did you send me a greeting gift regarding the festival. It was just 30 minas of gold that you sent me. My gift does not equal what I have given you every year.

I have built a new house. In my house, I have built a large [...damaged text...]. Your messengers have seen inside the house and the [...damaged text...], and are pleased. Now I am going to have a house opening. Come to eat and drink with me. I will not act as you did. 25 men and 25 women, 50 altogether in my service I send in regards to the house opening.

[...damaged text...] 10 wooden chariots, and 10 teams of horses I also send to you as your greeting gift.

EA 4: Royal deceit and threats

[...damaged text...] moreover, you, my brother, when I wrote to you about marrying your daughter in accordance with your practice of not giving a daughter, wrote to me saying, "From time immemorial no daughter of the king of Egypt is ever given to anyone."

Why not? You are king, so you do as you please! If you gave me a daughter, who would say anything?

After I was told this message, I wrote the following to my brother, "Someone's adult daughters who are beautiful women must be available. Send me a beautiful woman as your daughter. Who is going to say she is no daughter of the king? Yet keeping to the decision, you have not sent me anyone! You did not seek brotherhood and amity and so wrote to me about marriage that we might come closer to each other. Didn't I, for my part, write to you about marriage for this very reason, brotherhood and amity, that we might come closer to each other? Why then did my brother not send me just one woman? Since you did not send me a woman, should I refuse you a woman just as you did to me and not send

EA 4: Royal deceit and threats

her? But my daughters being available I will not refuse to you."

Perhaps also, when I wrote you about marriage and when I wrote to you about the animals [...damaged text...] Now, you need not accept the offspring as my daughter whom I will send to you, but return to me any animals requested by you.

As for the gold I wrote to you about, send me whatever is on hand, as much as possible before your messenger comes to me right now in all quickly this summer either in the month of Tammuz[1] or in the month Ab[2] so I can finish the work I am intent on. If during this summer in the months of Tammuz or Ab you send the gold I wrote to you about, I will give you my daughter. So please send the gold you wish to, but if in the months of Tammuz or Ab you do not send me the gold, and with it, I do not finish the work I am engaged in, what would be the point of your being pleased to send me gold? Once I have finished the work I am engaged in, what need would I have of gold? Then even if you send me 3000 talents of gold, I would not accept it, and I

EA 4: Royal deceit and threats

would send it back to you and not give you my daughter in marriage.

EA 2 Notes

1 Cuneiform: Dumuzu (𒇹𒈾)

Dumuzu was the equivalent of the modern Arabic and Hebrew month of Tammuz (تَمُّوز / תמוז), and late-June/early-July on the Gregorian calendar.

2 Cuneiform: Abu (𒇹𒉈)

Abu was the equivalent of the modern Arabic and Hebrew month of Ab (אב / آب), and late-July/early-August on the Gregorian calendar.

EA 5: Gifts of Egyptian Furniture for the Babylonian Palace

Tell the Great King Amenhotep III of Egypt:

A message from King Kadashman-Enlil of Babylon, your brother.

All goes well for me. May all go well for you. May all go well for your household, your wives, your sons, your officials, your infantry, your cavalry, your chariotry, and in your territories.

Al goes well for me, and all goes exceedingly well for my household, my wives, my sons, my officials, my extensive infantry, my cavalry, my chariotry, and in my territories.

I have recently heard that you have built some new quarters. I am sending with this message some furnishings for your house. I will also be preparing everything possible before the arrival of your messenger who is bringing your daughter. When your messenger returns, I will send them to you. I also sent to you with this message, in the charge of Shutti, a greeting-gift for the new house:

- 1 ebony bed inlaid with ivory and gold,

EA 5: Gifts of Egyptian Furniture for the Babylonian Palace

- 3 ebony beds inlaid with gold,
- 1 ebony headboard[1] inlaid with gold,
- 1 large ebony chair inlaid with gold.

The weight of all the gold in these things was 7 minas, along with 9 shekels of silver. Also, 10 ebony footrests inlaid with gold, and ivory footrests inlaid with gold, and [... damaged text...] of gold.

[... damaged text...] minas, 17 shekels of gold.

EA 5 Notes

1 Cuneiform: Uruššu (𒄰𒌓𒋗)

Translation: wooden headrest. (H. Ranke, *Keilschriftliches Material zur Altägyptischen Vokalisation* – 1910)

EA 6: Burna-Buriash II assumes the Throne of Babylon

Tell Amenhotep III, the king of Egypt, my brother:

A message from King Burra-Buriyash II[1] of Babylon, your brother.

All is well with me. May all be well with you, your household, your wives, your sons, your country, your officials, your cavalry, and your chariotry.

As you and my father were friendly to one another before, you and I should be friendly to one another. Between us, anything else what-so-ever should not be considered. Write to me, and ask for whatever you want from my country so that it may be taken to you, and I will write to you of what I want from your country so that it may be brought to me. [... damaged text...] I will trust you [... damaged text...] Write to me so that it may be taken to you, and as your greeting gift [... damaged text...] I send you.

EA 6 Notes

1 Cuneiform: ^{An}Buriiaáš (𒀭𒁍𒌨𒊏𒅀𒀸)

Burra-Buriyash was the King of Babylonia circa 1359–1333 BC.

EA 7: A Lesson in Geography

Tell Akhenaten, King of Egypt, my brother:

A message from the Great King Burra-Buriyash II, the king of Babylon, your brother.

All is very well for me and my household, my cavalry, my chariotry, my officials, and my country.

May all be very well for my brother and his household, his cavalry, his chariotry, his officials, and his country.

From the time the messenger of my brother arrived here, I have not been well, and so on no occasion has his messenger eaten or drank alcohol in my company. If you ask your messenger he will tell you I have not been well. As for my recovery is concerned, I am still by no means healthy. Furthermore, since I was not well and my brother showed no concern, I for my part, became angry with my brother saying "Has my brother not heard that I am ill? Why has he shown me no concern? Why has he sent no messenger here to visit me?"

My brother's messenger addressed me, saying "It's not a nearby place for him to hear about you,

EA 7: A Lesson in Geography

and send you greetings. The country is far away. Who is going to tell your brother so he might immediately send you greetings? Would your brother hear that you are ill and still not send you his messenger?"

I for my part asked him, "For my brother, a great king, is there really a distant country and a near-by one?"

He for his part answered me as follows, "Ask your own messenger whether the country is far away, and as a result, your brother did not hear about you and did not send anyone to greet you?"

When I asked my own messenger and he answered me that the journey is far, and I was no longer angry, and I no longer said, "As I am told everything that happens in my brother's country, and he wants for nothing. Furthermore, in my country everything is available and I want for absolutely nothing also, yet we have inherited long standing good relations from earlier kings, so we should send greetings to each other, should these same relations continue between us?"

I shall send my greetings to you, and your greetings you shall send to me [...damaged text...]

EA 7: A Lesson in Geography

My greetings [...damaged text...] and your greetings [...damaged text...]

Now, before sending him on his way, you have detained my messenger for two years, yet I spoke to your messenger and sent him on his way. Speak to my messenger immediately so he may come to me! Furthermore, as I am also told the journey is difficult, the rain has stopped and the weather is hot, so I am not sending many beautiful greeting-gifts. I send to my brother four minas of lapis-lazuli as a routine greeting-gift. In addition, I send my brother five teams of horses. As soon as the weather improves, my next messenger to come will bring many beautiful greeting-gifts to my brother. Furthermore, whatever my brother wants, let him just write to me so it might be taken from the palace.

Being engaged in a project, I request of my brother, could my brother send me a great deal of fine gold to use in my project. Yet the gold my brother sent me, my brother should not turn over into the charge of any deputy. My brother should personally check and then my brother should seal it and send it to me. Certainly, my brother did not check the earlier gold sent by my brother to me.

EA 7: A Lesson in Geography

It was only a deputy of my brother who sealed and sent it to me. When I put the 40 minas of gold that was brought to me into a kiln not even 10 appeared. I swear!

Furthermore, twice has a caravan of Ṣalmu my messenger who I sent to you been robbed. The first one by Biriyawaza,[1] and his second caravan by Pamachu a vassal governor of yours robbed us. When is my brother going to adjudicate this case? As my messenger spoke before my brother, so may Ṣalmu now speak before my brother? His property should be restored to him and he should be compensated for his losses.

EA 7 Notes

1 Cuneiform: Biriiaúza (𒁉𒊑𒅀𒌑𒍝)

Biriyawaza was the local governor of the Egyptian New Kingdom Syrian territories under Akhenaten. It is believed by was based out of Damascus. Biriyawaza was a Mitannian or Hyksos name.

EA 8: Problems in Canaan

Tell Akhenaten,[1] king of Egypt, my brother:

A message from the Great King Burra-Buriyash II, the king of Babylon, your brother.

For me, all is well. For you your country, your household, your wives, your sons, your officials, your cavalry, and your chariotry, may all is very well.

My brother and I made a mutual declaration of friendship and this is what we said, "Just as our fathers were friends with one another, so we will also be friends with one another. Now my merchants who were on their way with Achu-tabu were detained in Canaan for business matters. After Achu-tabu went to my brother in Hannathon,[2] Canaan, Shum-Adda the son of Balumme and Satatna the son of Sharatum of Acre[3] having sent men there, killed my merchants, and took away their money.

I send [...damaged text...] urgently. Ask him so that he may inform you of Canaan, which is your country and its kings are your servants. In your country, I have been robbed! Bring them to justice and make compensation for the money

EA 8: Problems in Canaan

they took away! Execute the men who put killed my servants and avenge my blood. If you don't put these men to death, they are going to kill again. Perhaps it will be a caravan of mine, or your own messengers, and so messengers between will be cut-off!

If they try and deny this to you, Shum-Adda blocked the passage of one man of my men, and detained him in his company, while another man was forced into the service of Satatna of Acre and is still serving him! These men should be brought to you so you can investigate and inquire whether they are dead, and thereby become informed.

As a greeting gift. I send to you one mina of lapis-lazuli. Send my messenger back immediately so I may know my brother's decision. Do not detain my messenger. Let him be off to me immediately.

EA 8 Notes

1 Cuneiform: Napùruriia (𒀀𒉽𒌉𒊑𒅀)

This is accepted by Egyptologists as a reference to Nefer Kheperu Ra (𓄤𓆣𓂋𓇳), the prenomen of Amenhopet IV, before he changed his name to Akhenaten.

2 Cuneiform: Ḫinatuna (𒌷𒄭𒈾𒌷)

The city also mentioned in the Book of Joshua, chapter 19, as Hannathon (Ενναθωθ / חַנָּתֹן), which is the more common name and used in this translation. The city is believed to have been at the site of Tel Hanaton (תל חנתון / Tal Badawiye (جبل تل بدويه) in northern modern Israel. It is theorized that the Egyptian pronunciation of the city's name was Khanaton.

3 Cuneiform: Agka (𒌷𒀝𒅗)

This is considered the Cuneiform transliteration of Acre (עַכּוֹ / عكّا), the coastal city in northern modern Israel. The city was recorded as Ôkå (𓉻𓂝𓂝𓏤) in the Middle Kingdom Excecration Texts, and as Ôåqå (זבל) in Demotic Egyptian during the early iron age.

EA 9: Ancient loyalties, new request

Tell Tutankhaten,[1] the king of Egypt, my brother:

A message from Burna-Buriash II, the king of Babylon, your brother.

All is well for me. May all go very well for you, your household, your wives, your sons, your country, your officials, your cavalry, your chariotry.

From the time my ancestors and your ancestors, a mutual declaration of friendship was made. They sent beautiful greeting-gifts to each other, and refused no request for anything beautiful. My brother has now sent me 2 minas of gold as my greeting-gift. If gold is plentiful, send me as much as your ancestors sent, but if it is scarce, send me half of what your ancestors sent. Why have you sent me 2 minas of gold? At the moment, my work on a temple is extensive, and I am quite busy carrying it out. Send me a great deal of gold, and for your part, whatever you want from my country, write to me so that it may be taken to you.

EA 9: Ancient Loyalties, New Request

In the time of Kurigalzu I,[2] my ancestor, all the Canaanites wrote here to him, saying, "Come to the frontiers of the country so we can revolt and ally with you!"

My ancestor sent them this reply, "Forget about being allied with me. If you become enemies of the king of Egypt, and are allied with anyone else, won't I then come and plunder you? How can there be an alliance with me?"

For the sake of your ancestor, my ancestor did not listen to them. Now, as for my Assyrian vassals,[3] I was not the one who sent them to you. Why have they come to your country on their own authority? If you love me, they will conduct no business whatsoever. Send them back to me empty-handed.

I send to you as your greeting-gift 3 minas of genuine lapis lazuli, and 5 teams of horses for 5 wooden chariots.

EA 9 Notes

1 Cuneiform: Nibḫipirura ()

This is accepted as the cuneiform spelling of Neb Kheperu Ra (), the prenomen of Tutankhaten, later known as Tutankhamen.

2 Cuneiform: Kurigalzu ()

Kurigalzu I was the 17th king of the Kassite Dynasty in Babylon. He ruled until circa 1375 BC, and was responsible for the building of the Fortress of Kurigalzu (Dur-Kurigalzu), which served as the capital of the Kassite Dynasty. It is believed that he conquered Elam circa 1400 BC, however, it is unclear when he assumed the throne in Babylonia.

3 This is a reference to King Ashur-uballit I's representatives that were sent to open diplomatic relations with Egypt. Ashur-uballit I ruled Assyria between 1365 and 1330 BC, after inheriting the kingdom from his father Eriba-Adad I, who had rebelled from the Mitannian Empire with the support of the Babylonians. Babylonian claims to Assyria evaporated quickly during Ashur-uballit I's reign.

EA 10: Egyptian Gold and Carpenters

Tell Tutankhaten, the king of Egypt:

A message from King Burna-Buriash II of Babylon.

All is well for me. May all be very well for you, your household, your wives, your sons, your officials, your infantry, your chariotry, your cavalry, and for your country.

From the time of Karaindash,[1] the messengers of your ancestors came regularly to my ancestors, until today, and they have been friends. Now, although you and I are friends, 3 times your have messengers come to me, and you have not sent to me a single beautiful greeting-gift, nor have I for my part sent you a beautiful greeting-gift.

As for your messenger, whom you sent to me, the 20 minas of gold that were brought here were not all there. When they put it into the kiln, only 5 minas of gold appeared. The residue that did appear when cooling off looked like ashes. Was the gold ever identified?

[...text damaged...] friends with [...text damaged...]

EA 10: Egyptian Gold and Carpenters

[...text damaged...] of a wild ox for [...text damaged...] when your messenger [...text damaged...] let him bring to me. There are skilled carpenters where you are. Let them represent a lifelike wild animal, land or aquatic, so that the hide is exactly like that of a living animal, and let your messenger bring it to me. But if there are some old ones already on hand, then as soon as Shindishugab, my messenger, reaches you, let him immediately rush, borrowing a chariot, to return here. Let them make some new ones for future delivery, and then when my messenger comes here with your messenger, let them bring them together.

I send as your greeting-gift 2 minas of lapis lazuli, and concerning your daughter Mayati, having heard about her, I send to her as her greeting-gift, a necklace of 1048 cricket-shaped gems of lapis-lazuli. And when your messenger comes along with Shindishugab I will make [...text damaged...] and have it brought to her.

EA 10 Notes

1 Cuneiform: Karaindaaš (𒅗𒊏𒅔𒁕𒀸)

King Karaindash was the Kassite king of Babylonia, Akkad, and Sumer circa 1410 BC.

EA 15: Assyria Joins the International Scene

Tell the king of the land of Egypt:

A message from Ashur-uballit I,[1] the king of the land of the god Ashur.

May all be well for you, your household, your land, your chariotry, and your infantry.

I have sent my messenger to you to visit you and to visit your land. Up to now, my predecessors have not written. Today, I have written to you. I send you a splendid chariot, 2 horses, and 1 date-stone of genuine lapis lazuli as your greeting gift.

Don't delay the messenger that I have sent to visit you. He should visit and then return here. He should see what you are like and what your land is like, and then return here.

EA 15 Notes

1 Cuneiform: Aššuruballita (𒀸𒋩𒌑𒁁𒇷𒀉𒋫)

King Ashur-uballit I ruled Assyria between 1353 and 1330 BC.

EA 19: Love and Gold

Tell Amenhotep III, Great King, the king of Egypt, my brother, my son-in-law, who loves me, and whom I love:

A message from the Great King Tushratta of the Mitanni, your father-in-law and brother, who loves you.

All is well for me. May all be well for you, for your household, for my sister, and for the rest of your wives, and your sons. May all be extremely well for your chariotry, your cavalry, your infantry, and for your country, and whatever else belongs to you.

Since the time of your ancestors, they always showed love to my ancestors. You went even further and showed greater love for my father. Now, in keeping with our constant and mutual love, you have made it ten times greater than the love shown to my father. May the gods grant it, and may Teshub,[1] my lord, and Amen and Teshub, my lords, and Amen make this mutual love of ours flourish forever, just as it is now.

When my brother sent Mane, his messenger, saying, "Send your daughter here to be my wife

EA 19: Love and Gold

and the mistress of Egypt," I caused my brother no distress and immediately I said, "Certainly!"

The one whom my brother requested I showed to Mane, and he saw her. When he saw her, he praised her greatly. I will send her in safety to my brother's country. May Shaushka[2] and Amen make her the image of my brother's desire.

Keliya, my messenger, brought my brother's words to me, and when I heard, they were very pleasing, and I rejoiced greatly, saying, "Certainly there is this between us! We love each other!"

Now, with such words let us love forever.

When I wrote to my brother, "Certainly, let's love very, very much, and between us let there be friendship."

I also said to my brother, "Certainly my brother, treat me ten times better than he did my father."

I also asked my brother for much gold saying, "Certainly, my brother grant me more than you did to father and send it to me. You sent my father much gold. You sent him large gold jars

EA 19: Love and Gold

and gold jugs. You sent gold ingots as if they were the cost of copper."

When I sent Keliya to my brother, I asked for gold saying, "Certainly my brother, treat me better than you did my father, and may you send much gold that has not been worked."

EA 19 Notes

1 Cuneiform: Teeššeub (𒀭𒅎𒌑𒁁)

This is considered a spelling variant of Teshub, the Hurrian god of the sky, thunder, and storms.

2 Cuneiform: Šauška (𒀭𒈹𒍑𒃲)

Shaushka was the Hurrian goddess of fertility and healing.

EA 23: A Goddess Travels to Egypt

Tell Amenhotep III, the king of Egypt, my brother and son-in-law, who I love and who loves me:

A message from King Tushratta of the Mittani, your father-in-law, who loves you.

All is well with me. May all be well with you, your household, and for Tadu-Heba, my daughter, your wife, who you love. May all be well with your wives, and your sons. May all be exceedingly well with your officials, your chariotry, your cavalry, your infantry, your country, and for whatever else belongs to you.

Shaushka of Nineveh, mistress of all lands says: "I wish to go to Egypt, a country that I love, and then return."

Now I send her with this message, and she is on her way. In the time of my father she went to your country, and just as before she dwelt there and they honored her, may my brother now honor her 10 times more than before. May my brother honor her, and at his pleasure let her go so that she may come back.

EA 23: A Goddess Travels to Egypt

May Shaushka, the mistress of heaven, protect us, my brother and me, for 100,000 years, and may our mistress grant both of us great joy. And let us act as friends.

Shaushka is for me my only deity, and is she not the deity of my brother?

EA 26: To the Queen Mother: Some Missing Gold Statues

Tell Tiye, the Mistress of Egypt:

A message from King Tushratta of the Mittani.

All is well for me. May all be well for you, your household, your sons. May all be well for Tadu-Heba, my daughter, your daughter-in-law. May all be very well for your countries, your infantry, and for whatever else belongs to you.

You are someone that knows that I always showed love to Amenhotep III, your husband, and Amenhotep III, your husband also showed always love to me. The things that I would write and say to Amenhotep III, your husband, and the things that Amenhotep III, your husband, would always write and say to me, you, Keliya, and Mane know. But you are the one, on the other hand, who knows much better than all others the things that we said to one another. No one else knows them.

Now, you said to Keliya, "Say to your lord, 'Amenhotep III, my husband, always showed love to your father and maintained it for you, and he did not forget his love for your father, and he did

EA 26: To the Queen Mother: Some Missing Gold Statues

not cut off the embassies that he had been accustomed to sending, one after the other. Now you are the one that must not forget your love for Amenhotep III, your brother. Increase it for Akhenaten and maintain it for him. You must keep on sending embassies of joy, one after the other. Do not end off.'"

"I won't forget the love for Amenhotep III, your husband. More than ever before, at this very moment, I show 10 times as much love to Akhenaten, your son. You are the one who knows the words of Amenhotep III, your husband, but you did not send all of my greeting-gift that your husband ordered to be sent. I had asked your husband for statues of solid gold, when I said, 'May my brother send me as my greeting gift statues of solid gold and [...damaged text...] of gold and genuine lapis lazuli.'"

"Yet now Akhenaten, your son, has coated statues of wood. With gold being like dirt in your son's country. Why have they been a source of such distress to your son that he has not given them to me? Furthermore, I asked [...damaged text...] to give this. Is this love? I had said,

EA 26: To the Queen Mother: Some Missing Gold Statues

"Akhenaten, my brother, is going to treat me 10 times better than his father did?" But now he has not given me even what his father was accustomed to give. Why have you not told Akhenaten the words that you yourself, and with your own mouth, said to me? If you do not tell them to him, and you keep quiet, can anyone else know? Let Akhenaten give me statues of solid gold! He must cause me no distress whatsoever, or [...damaged text...]. Let him treat me 10 times better than his father did, with love and evidence of esteem."

"May your own messengers go regularly with the messengers of Akhenaten, with 5 [...damaged text...] to Yuni, my wife, and may the messengers of Yuni, my wife, go regularly to you.

I send as your greeting-gift with this message, scent containers filled with sweet oil, and 1 set of stones.

EA 34: The Pharaoh's Reproach Answered

[...damaged text...]

A message from the king of Alashiya,[1] your brother.

Tell the king of the land of Egypt, my brother:

Know that at this time peace is in my land, and I bow to you seven times, and another seven times, and address you.

May your house be peaceful, and the house of your sons, your wives, your cavalry, your chariotry, and all your great lands. May there be peace for you my brother.

I set before myself every day, never wavering, your messenger for our counterpart to hold-back Ra!

Worthy and not listen to the roaring and never doing evil to anyone in their heart.

And the Pharaoh's voice was obeyed and now the Sun is like Ba'al!

Send a counterpart for our messenger my Equal!

EA 34 Notes

1 Cuneiform: Alašiia (𒀀𒆷𒅆𒅀)

- Translation: Alashiya

The Kingdom of Alashiya was mentioned in many texts from the late bronze age. Based on chemical analysis of the clay tablets sent from Alashiya to other kingdoms during the bronze age, is believed to have been in southern Cyprus, spanning the region where the cities of Kalavasos (Καλαβασός) and Alassa (Ἄλασσα) are located today. The name of Alassa is probably descended from Alashiya. This kingdom would have been west of the kingdom of Kåtjåy (𒃰𒋾𒅀) / Kt (𓎡𓏏) / Kty (^𝑛𝑦), later known as Citium (Κίτιον), indicating that it did not rule all of Cyprus at the time. During the bronze age, Alashiya also corresponded with the Mycenaean Greeks who recorded the name as Arasijo (𐀀𐀣𐀯𐀍), and the Ugaritic Canaanites who recorded the name as Åltٍy (𐎀𐎍𐎘𐎊).

EA 35: The Hand of Ammit

Tell the king of Egypt, my brother:

A message from the king of Alashiya, your brother.

All is well for me, and my household, my wives, my sons, my officials, my horses, my chariotry. All is very well in my country.

May all be well for my brother, and for your household, your wives, your sons, your officials, your cavalry, your chariotry, and in your country, may all go very well. My brother, I send my messenger with your messenger to Egypt. I send 500 measures of copper to you with my messenger, as my brother's greeting-gift.

My brother, do not be concerned that the amount of copper is small. The hand of Ammit[1] is now in my country, who has slain all the men of my country, and there are not copper-smiths left. So, my brother, do not be concerned. Send your messenger with my messenger immediately, and I will send you whatever copper you request, my brother.

My brother, will you send me extremely large quantities of silver? My brother, give me the

EA 35: The Hand of Ammit

very best silver, and then I will send you, my brother, whatever you request. Moreover, my brother, give me the ox that my messenger requests. Also, my brother, and send me two canteens[2] of "sweet oil," my brother, and send me one of the experts in vulture augury.[3]

Moreover, my brother, the men in my country keep asking me about the timber that the king of Egypt received from me. My brother, the payment is due.

EA 35 Notes

1 Cuneiform: ^{an}Mašmaš (✳-┼-┼)

• Pronounciation: ^{an}āšipu in Old Akkadian, ^{an}Barbar in Babylonian, or Ånṭṭ in Canaanite

The translation of ^{an}Mašmaš as 'Nergal' is commonly used by Egyptologists, however, Nergal was spelled ^{an}Gìrunuggal (✳-◯▷-◁◰-) in Old Assyrian and Old Babylonian. Both Nergal and ^{an}Mašmaš were listed in the Neo-Assyrian God List uncovered in the ruins of Nineveh, meaning that the Assyrians considered them separate gods. Given that the king of Alashiya was trying to blame a 'god of death' for his country's sudden decline in copper production, it is unlikely that he would have referred to an obscure Assyrian god, for whom almost no mention of has survived to the present. ^{an}Mašmaš was likely an attempt to write the name of Ammit, the Egyptian New Kingdom era "goddess of the dead." She was a new god, based on the Hyksos era Canaanite god ^{an}Mwt (✳-─-◁), who had replaced Khonsu as the god that disposed of the bodies of the dead in northern Egypt. Ammit's name had not been standardized by the New Kingdom, and was variously written as Ôm-mwt (𓌳𓃀𓏏𓅓), Ôm-mwt (𓌳𓃀𓏏𓅓), Ôm-mt (𓌳𓃀𓏏), Ôm-mt (𓌳𓃀𓏏), Ôåm-myt (𓌳𓃀𓏭𓏏), Ôm-myt (𓌳𓏭𓏏), Ômt-mwt (𓌳𓏏𓃀𓅓), and Ômå-myt (𓌳𓏭𓏏).

An alternate translation of the cuneiform word might be something to the effect of 'high enchanters' or 'sacred magicians,' based on the Old Akkadian translation of āšipu (┼-┼). The term āšipu remained in use in Syria throughout history, as a term refering to 'enchanters,' as reflected in

EA 35 Notes

the Hebrew ashaf (אָשַׁף), and Syriac ashshafa (ܐܫܦܐ). This alternate reading would suggest that king of Alashiya was blaming sorcerers instead of a god for the plague in his land, however, as the Assyrians recorded ^{an}Mašmaš as the name of a god, this seems unlikely.

As Egyptologists agree that a 'god of the dead,' is being refered to, the more likely translation of Ammit is used over the more common choice of Nergal.

2 Cuneiform: Quqquba (𒄀𒁁𒁁𒄑)

The quqquba was a small flask or jar, originally a canteen made from an animal's stomach.

3 Bird augury was commonly practiced in North Africa, the Middle East, and the Mediterranean Sea until the rise of Christianity. Bird augurs would watch the flight of birds to interpret messages from the sky-gods. In Roman mythology, the founders of Rome, Romulus and Remus, chose the location of Rome based on vulture augury.

EA 38: A Brotherly Quarrel

Tell the King of Egypt, my brother:

A message from the king of Alashiya, your brother.

All is well for me, and may all be well for you, your household, your chief wives, your sons, your cavalry, your chariotry, and your numerous infantry. May all be very well for your country and officials.

Why, my brother, do you ask me, "Does my brother not know this?"

As far as I am concerned, I have done nothing of the sort! Indeed, men of Lycia[1] come every year and seize villages in my country.

My brother, you say to me, "Men from your country were with them."

My brother, I myself do not know that they were with them. If men from my country were, send them back and I will act as I see fit. You yourself do not recognize men from my country. They would not do such a thing! But if men from my country did do this, then you yourself may do as you see fit. Now, my brother, since you have not sent back my messenger, for this tablet it is

EA 38: A Brotherly Quarrel

the king's brother sent as a messenger. Let him write. Your messengers must tell me what I am to do.

[...damaged text...]

Furthermore, which ancestors of yours did such a thing to my ancestors? Don't answer, my brother, and do not be concerned.

EA 38 Notes

1 Cuneiform: Lukaki (𒇻𒋻)

Lukaki, also transliterated as Lukka or Lukki, is believed to have been the Cuneiform spelling of Lycia, an ancient kingdom in southwest Anatolia. The expanse of the Lukaki lands at the time is unclear, and some historians believe the controlled Lycaonia and Pisidia in addition to Lycia, in which case they would have dominated southwest Anatolia. They were allied with the Neshites (Hittites) against the Egyptians at the Battle of Kadesh in 1274 BC, however, fought against the Neshites in the 1180s, contributing to the collapse of the Neshite empire. During the 1100s, they attacked Egypt with the Sea Peoples, contributing to the collapse of the Egyptian New Kingdom.

EA 39: Duty-Free

Tell the king of Egypt, my brother:

A message from the king of Alashiya, your brother.

All is well for me, and may all be well for you, your household, your chief wives, your sons, your wives, your chariotry, and your extensive cavalry. May all be very well in Egypt.

My brother, let my messengers leave quickly and safely so that I may hear my brother's reply. These men are my merchants, my brother, so let them leave safely and quickly. No one making a claim in your name should approach the merchants from my ship.

EA 59: From the Citizens of Tunip

Tell the king of Egypt, our lord:

A message from the citizens of Tunip, your servant.

May all be well for you. We bow at the feet of my lord.

My lord, Tunip, your servant says:

Who ruled Tunip in the past? Didn't Thutmose III[1] your forefather rule it?

The gods, and the Syrian governor[2] of the king of Egypt, our lord, lives in Tunip, and he should inquire about his forefathers when we did not belong to our lord, the king of Egypt.

Now, for 20 years, we have gone on writing to the king, our lord, but our messengers have stayed on with the king, our lord. And now, our lord, we ask for the son of Aki-Teshshup from the king, our lord. May our lord return him. My lord, if the king of Egypt has sent the son of Aki-Teshshup, why does the king, our lord, call him back from the journey?

Now, Aziru[3] is going to hear that in Hittite territory a hostile fate has defeated your servant,

EA 59: From the Citizens of Tunip

your gardener. Should his infantry and his chariotry be delayed, Aziru will do to us just as he did to Nii. If we ourselves are negligent and the king of Egypt does nothing about these things that Aziru is doing, then he will surely turn his hand against our lord. When Aziru entered Sumur,[4] he did to them as he pleased, even in the palace of the king, our lord. Yet our lord did nothing about these things.

Now your city Tunip weeps, and its tears flow, and there is no grasping of our hand. We have continued writing to the king, our lord, the king of Egypt, for 20 years, and not a single word of our lord has reached us.

EA 59 Notes

1 Cuneiform: Manaḫpiia (𒀀𒀀𒀀𒀀𒀀)

This is accepted as the Cuneiform spelling of Men Kheper Ra (𒀀𒀀𒀀), Thutmose III's prenomen. Tunip, a town near Hama in Syria was part of Thutmose III's empire in the 1400s BC.

2 Cuneiform: Naaḫri illaan (𒀀𒀀𒀀𒀀 𒀀𒀀𒀀𒀀)

The term Naahri appears to be the Cuneiform equivalent to the Aramaic Nhriim (𐡍𐡄𐡓𐡉𐡌) and Syriac Nahrayn (ܢܗܪܝܢ), which was also the Egyptian name for the region of western Syria that they ruled at the time. The term Illaan appears to be a Cuneiform spelling of the Aramaic word meaning 'governor(s),' or 'administrator(s),' virtually identical to the Arabic word åwlawn (أُوَلَوْن).

3 Cuneiform: Aziru (𒀀𒀀𒀀)

Aziru was the local governor of the Amorite land of Amurru, in northern modern Lebanon and western Syria.

4 Cuneiform: Simirra (𒀀𒀀𒀀𒀀)

Sumur was a city on the Mediterranean coast of modern Syria, believed to have been at the site of Tell Kazel. The city's name is also transliterated as Simirra, Simyra, Simura, Sumra, Sumura, Sumuru, Zemar, Zimirra, or Zimyra.

EA 75: Political Chaos

Tell the lord king of the lands:

A message from Rib-Hadda.

The mistress of the city-state of Byblos proclaims the strength of my Lord!

I fall at the feet of my Lord the Sun-God. I bow before you seven times, and another seven times.

Know, my King Lord that since all eternity the city of Byblos has been peaceful in the hands of your servant, however, now there is warfare with the army of the Habiru[1] [...text damaged...]

EA 75 Notes

1 Cuneiform: Habirus (𒄩𒁉𒊒𒈨𒌍)

The exact nature of the Habirus is unclear, and it is debated how much they are related to the Hebrews. The Amarna Letters do mention the Habirus being in some of the same locations mentioned in the Books of Joshua and Judges, and does mention a Habiru named Joshua, however, this is unlikely to have been the Biblical Joshua, as he would have lived either a century earlier (Septuagint's chronology), or a century later (Masoretic chronology). The difficulty identifying the Habirus with the Hebrews, is due to records from the Babylonians and Assyrians, regarding the Habirus plundering their regions as well, from the 1800s BC through the 1400s BC. While all of these attacks cannot be associated with Joshua's invasion of Canaan, they do generally correlate with the movement of Terah and his sons out of Ur circa 2100 BC (Septuagint's chronology). In the Hebrew Book of Genesis, Terah, the father of Abram, was recorded as being a fifth-generation descendant of Eber, the patriarch of all Hebrews, which implies there were a large number of Hebrews by the time that Terah left Ur, which would explain the rest of the Habirus.

EA 86: Complaint to an Official

Tell Amenappa:

A message from Rib-Hadda.

I bow. May Amen, your lord, establish your honor before of the king, your lord pharaoh[1] my Lord.

Hear me! The war is severe, so come with armies of archers[2] that you may capture the land of Amurru. Day and night we have cried for you, and they say a great deal is taken by them to the land of Mitanni.

So now you must not ask, "Why should I come out?"

You have already said, "Yanhamu[3] sent you grain."

Have you not heard? A servant [...text damaged...]

Be informed that Ummahnu the servant of the Lady of Byblos, along with her husband Milkuru [...text damaged...]

So ask the king that it may be presented to the Lady. Don't hold anything back. Moreover, ask that grain, the product of the land of Yarimuta,[4]

EA 86: Complaint to an Official

be given to his servant, just as it was given to Sumur before, so we may remain alive until the king gives to his city. For 3 years, I have been repeatedly plundered of our grain. There is nothing to pay for horses.

Why should the king grant 30 pairs of horses, and you yourself take 10 pairs? If you take, take all of them, but let grain from the land of Yarimuta be given to us to eat.

Send ships so I myself can get [...damaged text...]

EA 86 Notes

1 Cuneiform: Šarri (⬤𒈗)

The term Sharri is believed to be the Cuneiform translation of 'Pharaoh,' as it could be translated as 'king-sun.'

2 Cuneiform: èrim meš pitati (𒂟 𒈨𒌍 𒉺𒋾𒋫𒋾)

The term èrimmeš pitati is used in many of the Amarna Letters, and based on context is accepted as 'armies of archers.' The term is similar to the Egyptian term heri-pedjet (𓂝 𓌢), which translates as 'above archer,' an Egyptian military rank. The addition of 'hero' (𒈨𒌍) in the middle, would render the term as 'above heroic archers,' however, in a mixed vocabulary, more indicative of the Canaanite and Hyksos dynasties than the New Kingdom era. It is likely the Cypriot scribe could not speak Egyptian.

3 Cuneiform: Iaanḫamumi (𒅀𒀭𒄩𒈬𒈪)

Yanhamu is the most common English transliteration of the name, however, Yenhamu and Enhamu are also used.

4 Cuneiform: Iarimuta (𒅀𒊑𒈬𒋫)

This name is generally transliterated as Yarimuta, and is likely the same location that was referred to as the home of 'the Habiru of Mount Yarmuta' in the stele of Seti I from circa 1280 BC. This name, like some other toponyms in the Amarna Letters includes a transliteration of the Egyptian word tâ (𓇾), meaning 'land,' indicating the name of the

EA 86 Notes

place was something like Iarimu. This location is also generally accepted as being Yarmus (יְרְמֹוּת) from the Hebrew book of Joshua, which the Greeks translated as Ierimouth (Ιεριμουθ) in the Septuagint. Yarmus/Ierimouth is generally identified as the archaeological site of Tel Jarmuth (Khirbet el-Yarmûk / Tel Yarmut). According to the Book of Joshua, prior to the Hebrews invading Canaan, Yarmus/Ierimouth, along with several other cities in the region were Amorite towns, however, the Hebrews conquered the region circa 1508 BC (Septuagint chronology), and slaughtered the Amorites that had been living there. If this story is factual, then Joshua's Hebrews were the Habiru that were living there during King Seti I's rule between 1290 and 1279 BC. It also means that the people living at Yarimuta that had been sending food to Byblos in the mid-1300s were Habiru/Hebrews.

EA 100: The City of Arqa to the King

This is a tablet from Arqa[1] to the king, our lord:

Message from Arqa and its elders. We bow at the feet of the king, our lord, seven times and, another seven times.

Tell our lord, the sun, a message from Arqa.

May the heart of the king, our lord, know that we guard Arqa for him. When the king, our lord, sent Dumubihaa, he told us, "A message from the king, 'Guard Arqa!' The sons of the traitor to the king seek our harm."

Arqa is loyal to the king.

In regards to silver that was given to Subaru along with 30 horses and chariots, may you know the mind of Arqa! When a tablet from the king arrived that instructed us to raid the lands that the Habiru had taken from the king when they waged war with us against the enemy of our lord, the man whom you placed over us. Vigilantly, we are guarding the land. May the king, our lord, listen to the words of his loyal servants.

May he grant a gift to his servants so our enemies will see this and eat dirt. May the breath of the king not depart from us. We shall keep the

EA 100: The City of Arqa to the King

city gate barred until the breath of the king reaches us. The war is severe against us! Terrible! Terrible!

EA 100 Notes

1 Cuneiform: Irkata (𒌷𒅕𒅗𒋫)

Like other topynoms in the Amarna Letters, this name ends with a transliteration of the Egyptian word tå (𓇿), meaning land, meaning the name of the land was Irka. This is accepted as being the cuneiform spelling of Arqa (عرقا), a town in northern Lebanon, in the Akkar governorate. The site of the old city is identified as the ruins of Tell Arqa today, which was inhabited since at least neolithic times.

EA 107: Charioteers, but no horses

Rib-Hadda says to his lord, king of all countries, the Great King, king of armies:

May the Lady of Byblos[1] grant power to the king, my lord. I bow at the feet of my lord, my sun, seven times and 7 another times.

Being a loyal servant of the king, the sun, with my mouth I tell important matters to the king that are nothing but the truth. May the king, my lord, listen to the words of his loyal servant. May the archer-commander stay in Sumur, but call Haapi to yourself and interrogate him, and find out about his actions. Then, if it pleases you, appoint as its commissioner, someone respected by the king's governors.

May my lord listen to my words. Seeing that Aziru, the son of Abdi-Asherah, is in Damascus, along with his brothers, send archers that they might capture him, and the land of the king be peaceful. If things go as they are now, Sumur will not stand. Moreover, may the king, my lord, hear the words of his loyal servant. There is no money to pay for horses. Everything is gone that might keep us alive. So send me 30 pairs of horses along with chariots. I have charioteers,[2] but I do not

EA 107: CHARIOTEERS, BUT NO HORSES

have horses to march against the enemies of the king. Therefore, I am afraid, and therefore, I have not gone to Sumur.

EA 107 Notes

1 Cuneiform: Kubla (𒆪𒌒𒆷)

Kubla is the ancient Cuneiform name of the city of Byblos (جبيل), in Lebanon. Byblos is one of the oldest continuously inhabited cities in the world, having been inhabited since at least 5000 BC. The Egyptian name since the Old Kingdom era had been Ka'ban (𓊡𓃀𓈖). Most European language names for the city are derived from the Greek name Byblos, which is based on the word for papyrus, as Byblos was the major transshipment point for Egyptian papyrus to the Aegean early in Greek civilization. The Arabic name of the city, Jubayl (جبيل), is derived from the ancient Canaanite name Gbl (𐤂𐤁𐤋), which is a later development of the term transliterated into Cuneiform in this letter.

2 Cuneiform: Marianuma (𒇽𒈨𒌍𒋗𒌋𒈠)

This word is the Cuneiform spelling of Maryannu, the word used across the Middle East and North Africa for 'charioteers,' from the Second Intermediate Period / Babylonian Dark Age onward. It is a Hurrianized Indo-Aryan term, derived from the Sanskrit 'marya' meaning 'young warrior,' with a Hurrian suffix.

EA 132: The Hope for Peace

Tell the king, my lord, my sun:

A message from Rib-Hadda, your servant. May the Lady of Byblos grant power to the king, my lord. I fall at the feet of my lord seven times and, another seven times.

May you consider Byblos, your loyal city. Earlier, Abdi-Asherah[1] attacked me, and I wrote to your father, "Send the royal archers, and the entire land will be recaptured in a day."

Did he not capture for himself Abdi-Asherah, together with his property? Now Aziru has gathered all the Habirus and has said to them, "If Gubla is not [...text damaged...]"

Look, Yanhamu is with you, ask him if I did not tell him, "If you make an alliance [...text damaged...] with the sons of Abdi-Asherah, they will capture for you as a prisoner."

He listened to me, and he guarded the cities of the king, his lord. I said the same thing to Pawura so he would not listen to the words of Haapi, whose father turned the cities into enemies. Now Haapi has surrendered Sumur. May the king not neglect this action, since a commissioner was

EA 132: The Hope for Peace

killed. If now you are negligent, then Pahura will not stay in Kamid al lawz,[2] and all your governors will be killed. I keep writing like this to the palace, but no attention is paid to me. Send ships to fetch the Lady's property and me. Send 50 to 100 men, and 50 to 100 Harappan men,[3] 50 chariots, to guard the city for you. Send archers and bring peace to the land.

EA 132 Notes

1 Cuneiform: árad Ašiirta (𒀴𒀸𒉌𒅕𒋫)

- Translation: slave of Astarte
- Pronouciation: Abdi-Ashirta (in Aramaic)

Abdi-Ashirta was the Amorite ruler of Amurru who was in conflict with King Rib-Hadda of Byblos. Both were subject to the New Kingdom, however, they appear to have raided each other's territories regularly. The name Ashitra is accepted as an easlier spelling of Åštrt (𐤏𐤕𐤓𐤔𐤀) the Canaanite goddess the Greek Astártē (Ἀστάρτη) was based on. During the New Kingdom era, the goddess was known as Ôåstjr (𓉠𓊃𓏏𓂋) in Egyptian, although several variations of the spelling have been documented. Another equivalent goddess was the Mesopotamian Ishtar, however, Ishtar was spelled as ^{an}Inana (𒀭𒈹) in Sumerian, ^{an}Aštar (𒀭𒊨) in Akkadian, ^{an}Išdar (𒀭𒁯) in Amorite, Eštar (𒁯) in Neo-Sumerian, and Ištar (𒅖𒁯) in Assyrian and Babylonian, none of which matches the spelling in this letter.

2 Cuneiform: Kumidu (𒆪𒈪𒁺)

This is accepted as the ancient name of Kamid al lawz (كامد اللوز), a town in the Beqaa Valley of Lebanon.

3 Cuneiform: Melukhkha ki (𒁹𒈨𒈛𒆠)

Melukhkha^{ki} is generally translated as 'the land of Meluhha.' The location of Meluhha has been greatly debated in the past century, however, the current

EA 132 NOTES

consensus is that it was in ancient India or Pakistan. If this is the case, then there were ancient Indians serving in the Egyptian army for some reason. The term is believed to be related to the Sanskrit term Mleccha, which translates as 'non-Vedic,' but is only found in Indo-Aryan languages, not other Indo-European, or even Indo-Iranian languages, implying it was adopted from a non-Aryan people already living in South Asia. The word is not found in the early Vedas, but occurs for the first time in the late Vedic era text the Shatapatha Brahmana, dated to the 700s BC. There were Mleccha warriors in the Mahabharata, set circa 3150 BC, however, the surviving text of the Mahabharata is dated to the later Epic Sanskrit era, circa 300 BC.

Therefore, the likely translation of Meluhha, would have been 'Harappans' before the collapse of the Indus Civilization, circa 1300 BC, shortly after the era the letter was written in, and therefore that term is used in this translation. It is unclear why there would have been Harappans in the Egyptian army at the time. It is possible that the reference was not to Harappans, but the brown-skinned people from the Ethiopian Highlands and Eritrean coast-land, which the Egyptians were in contact with at the time, as it is believed the term Meluhha was applied to the region later in the Neo-Assyrian era, however, this is hypothetical in the mid-New Kingdom era, and as the Harappan civilization was still alive, that term is used in this translation.

EA 144: Zimreddi of Sidon to Pharaoh

Tell the king, my lord, my god, my sun, the breath of my life:

A message from Zimreddi, the mayor of Sidon. I bow at the feet of my lord, god, sun, the breath of my life, seven times and, another seven times.

May the king, my lord, know that Sidon, the servant of the king, my lord, which he put in my charge, is safe and sound.

When I heard the words of the king, my lord, when he wrote to his servant, then my heart rejoiced, and my head went high, and my eyes shone, at hearing the word of the king, my lord. May the king know that I have made preparations before the arrival of the archers of the king, my lord. I have prepared everything following the command of the king, my lord.

May the king, my lord, know that the war against me is very terrible. All the cities that the king put in my charge, have been taken by the Habiru. May the king put me in the charge of a man that will lead the archers of the king to call to account the cities that have been taken by the

EA 144: Zimreddi of Sidon to Pharaoh

Habiru, so you can restore them to my authority so I may be able to serve the king, my lord, like our ancestors before me.

EA 145: Word on Amurru

Tell the king, my lord:

A message from Zimreddi.

I fall at your feet. Know that I am safe and sound, and with your greeting from the presence of the king, my lord, you brought back to me the breath of his mouth.

I have heard your words that you sent me through [...damaged text...] The war is very severe. [...damaged text...]

The king, our lord, has indeed been earnestly addressed from his lands, but the breath of his mouth does not reach his servants that are in the countryside. Moreover, as to your orders in regards to the land of Amurru, "The word you hear from there, you must report to me," everyone has heard that [...damaged text...] he awaits you.

EA 147: A Hymn to the Pharaoh

Tell the king, my lord, my god, my sun:

A message from Abi-Ishki,[1] your servant. I fall at the feet of the king, my lord, seven times and, another seven times. I am the dirt under the sandals of the king, my lord.

My lord is the sun who comes out over all lands day by day, like the ways of the sun, his gracious father who gives life by his sweet breath and returns with his north wind, who establishes the entire land in peace, by the power of his arm Haapi, who speaks his voice from the sky like Ba'al, and all the land is frightened at his voice.

Your servant writes here to his lord, that he heard the gracious messenger of the king who came to his servant, and the sweet breath that came forth from the mouth of the king. My lord, his servant sends his breath came back!

Before the arrival of the messenger of the king, my lord, breath had not come back, and my nose was blocked. Now that the breath of the king has come out to me, I am very happy and my strength grows, day by day.

EA 147 Notes

1 Cuneiform: abi Ish ki (𒀀𒋾𒅖𒆠)
   - Translation: father devastator of land (or dusty land)

EA 149: Neither Water nor Wood

Tell the king, my lord, my sun, my god:

A message from Abi-Ishki, your servant. I bow at the feet of the king, my lord, seven times and, another seven times. I am the dirt under the feet and sandals of the king, my lord.

King, my lord, you are like the sun, like Ba'al in the sky. May the king give his thought to his servant. The king, my lord, charged me with guarding Tyre, the servant of the king, but after I wrote an express tablet to the king, my lord, he has not replied to me. I am a commissioner of the king, my lord, and I am one that reports both the good and bad news to the king, my lord. May the king send 20 palace attendants to guard his city so that I may go to the king, my lord, and see his face.

What is the life of a palace attendant when breath does not come out from the mouth of the king, his lord? He only lives if the king writes to his servant, and he lives forever.

For my part, since last year I have desired to go and see the face of the king, my lord, but Zimreddi, the prince intercepted me. He made

EA 149: Neither Water nor Wood

my caravan turn back from the king, my lord, saying, "Who can get you to the king?"

Listen, my lord! Aziru, the son of Abdi-Asherah, the rebel against the king, has seized Sumur.

Haapi [...damaged text...] gave Sumur to Aziru.

May the king not neglect this city and his land. When they hear the name of the king and the name of his army, they will be very afraid, and all the land will be afraid, those who do not obey the king, my lord. The king knows that you installed me as mayor in Tyre. Zimreddi seized Usu from his servant. I abandoned it, and so we have neither water nor wood. Nor is there a place where we can bury the dead. So may the king, my lord, give consider his servant.

The king, my lord, wrote to me on a tablet, "Write whatever you hear to the king."

Zimreddi of Sidon and Aziru rebel against the king, and the men of Arwada have exchanged oaths among themselves, and they have assembled their ships, chariotry, and infantry, to attack Tyre, the servant of the king.

EA 149: Neither Water nor Wood

If the powerful hand of the king comes, it will defeat them, and they will not be able to capture Tyre. They captured Sumur through the instructions of Zimreddi, who brings the instructions of the king to Aziru. I sent a tablet to the king, my lord, but he has not replied to his servant.

Since last year there has been war against me. There is no water, there is no wood. May he send a tablet to his servant permitting him to go in and see his face.

May the king consider his servant and his city, and may he not abandon his city and his land. Why should a major of the king, our lord, flee from the land? Zimreddi knows, and the traitor knows that the arm of the king is absent. Now, a palace attendant is bringing my tablet to the king, the sun lord, and may the king reply to his servant.

EA 153: Ships on Hold

Tell the king, my lord:

A message from Abi-Ishki, your servant. I fall at your feet seven times, and another seven times.

I have done what the king, my lord, ordered.

The entire country-side is afraid of the infantry of the king, my lord. I have had my men hold ships for the infantry of the king, my lord. Whoever has disobeyed has no family left alive.

Since I guard the city of the king, my lord, my safety is the king's responsibility. May he take consider his servant, who is on his side.

EA 154: Orders carried out

Tell the king, my lord:

A message from Abi-Ishki, your servant. I bow at the feet of the king, my lord, seven times, and another seven times. I am the dirt under the sandals of the king, my lord.

I have heard what the king wrote to his servant, "Let my forces be prepared against Yawa."

What the king ordered, that I have carried out with the greatest joy. Moreover, since the departure of the soldiers of the king, my lord, from me, the ruler of Sidon does not allow me or my people to go to land to harvest wood or to collect water for drinking. He has killed one man, and he has captured another.

May the king consider of his servant.

EA 156: Aziru in Amurru

Tell the king, my lord, my god, my sun:

A message from Aziru, your servant. I fall at the feet of my lord seven times, and another seven times.

Now, as to any request that the sun, my lord, makes, I am your servant forever, and my sons are your servants.

I send my two sons as attendants with this message, and they are to do what the king, orders. Only let him leave me in Amurru.

EA 158: Father and Son

Tell Tutu, my lord, my father:

A message from Aziru, your son, your servant. I fall at the feet of my father. For my father may all be well.

Tutu, I hereby grant the request of the king, my lord, and whatever may be the request of the king, my lord, he should write and I will grant it.

Moreover, as you in that place are my father, whatever may be the request of Tutu, my father, just write and I will grant it as you are my father and my lord, and I am your son, the land of Amurru is your land, and my house is your house. Write me any request at all of yours, and I will grant your every request.

You are in the personal service of the king, my lord. Sky forbid that treacherous men have spoken maliciously against me in the presence of the king, my lord, and you should not permit them. As you are in the personal service of the king, my lord, representing me, you should not permit malicious talk against me.

EA 158: Father and Son

I am the servant of the king, my lord, and I will not deviate from the orders of the king, my lord, or from the orders of Tutu, my father, ever.

If the king, my lord, does not love me and rejects me, then what am I to say?

EA 161: An Absence Explained

Tell the great king, my lord, my god, my sun:

A message from Aziru, your servant. I fall at the feet of my lord, my god, my sun, seven times, and another seven times.

My lord, I am your servant, and on my arrival in the presence of the king, my lord, I told my affairs in the presence of the king, my lord. My lord, do not listen to the treacherous men that denounce me in the presence of the king, my lord. I am your servant forever.

The king, my lord, has spoken about Hani. My lord, I was staying in the town of Tunip, and so I did not know that he had arrived. As soon as I heard, I went up after him, but I did not catch up to him. May Hani arrive safe and sound, so that the king, my lord, can ask him how I provided for him. My brothers and the Mitanni[1] were at his service. They gave oxen, sheep, and goats, and birds, his food and strong drink.

I gave horses and donkeys for his journey. May the king, my lord, hear my words. When I come to the king, my lord, Hani will go before me, and like a mother and like a father he will provide for

EA 161: An Absence Explained

me. Now my lord says, "You hid from Hani." However, may your gods and the Sun be witness, I was residing in Tunip.

The king, my lord, has spoken about the building of Sumur. The kings of Nuhashshe[2] have been at war with me and have captured my cities at the instruction of Hatip. So, I have not built it. Now, I am rushing to build it. And may my lord know that Hatip has taken half of the things that the king, my lord, gave to me. All the gold and silver that the king, my lord, gave me, Hatip has taken. May my lord know. Moreover, the king, my lord, also said, "Why did you provide for the messenger of the king of the Hittites, but did not provide for my messenger?" But this is the land of my lord, the king. My lord made me one of the mayors! Let my lord's messenger come to me so I can give all that I promised in the presence of the king, my lord. I will give food supplies, ships, oil, logs of boxwood, and various woods.

EA 161 Notes

1 Cuneiform: É An (𒂍𒀭).

- Translation: House of An (the sky), House of El

The 'dingir' (𒀭) symbol was used in Sumerian and Akkadian to denote the sky, the sky-father god An. In cuneiform texts originating in Canaan, it is accepted as a reference to El, the Canaanite sky-father god. The É (𒂍) was the cuneiform character meaning house, which results in the translation of 'Bet-ili' in most translations of the Amarna Texts, which is simply another transliteration of Bethel. A people known as the Bethanites (Βαιθανι) were mentioned in passing in the Septuagint's 1st Paralipomenon, however, mirrored by Mitni (מִתְנִי) in Divrei-hayYamim, suggesting this was the ultimate origin of the Septuagint's Eyaeon (Ευαῖον), which is mirrored by variations of Chivvi (חִוִּי) in the Masoretic text, both of which appear to be references to the Mitanni, and therefore "Mitanni" is used as a translation.

2 Nuhashshe was a state in northern Syria between the Euphrates and Orontes rivers, in the border-lands of the Egyptian and Hittite Empires at the time.

EA 164: Coming, on condition

Tell tutu, my lord, my father:

A message from Aziru, your servant. I bow at the feet of my lord.

Hatip has come, and brought the gracious and sweet words of the king, my lord, and I am quite overjoyed. My land, and my brothers, the servants of the king, my lord, and the servants of Tutu, my lord, are overjoyed when the breath of the king, my lord, comes. I do not deviate from the orders of my lord, my god, my sun, or from the orders of Tutu, my lord.

My lord, since Hatip is residing with me, he and I will make the journey. My lord, the king of the Hittites has come to Nuhashshe and I cannot go. If the king of the Hittites leaves immediately, I will travel with Hatip. May the king, my lord, hear my words.

My lord, I fear the king, my lord, and Tutu. Here before my gods, and my messenger, I would swear an oath before I make the journey to Tutu and the officials of the king, my lord. Therefore Tutu, the king, my lord, and the officials,

EA 164: Coming, on Condition

"We will not devise anything regarding Aziru that is not good."

Hereby you are sworn an oath by my gods and by Amen. Tutu, know that I will come to you.

EA 170: To Aziru in Egypt

Tell the king, our lord:

A message from Baaliah[1] and a message from Bethel. We bow at the feet of our lord. May all be well for our lord. All is well here in the lands of our lord.

Do not worry at all, our lord, or trouble yourself. Our lord, as soon as you can, meet with Zuzilamaan[2] so they will not remain there with you.

Moreover, Hittite soldiers, under the command of Lupakku, have captured the cities in the Beqaa Valley.[3] Our lord should also be informed that they captured Adummim[4] when they captured the cities.

Also, we have heard the following, "Zitana has come with 90,000 infantrymen," however, we have not confirmed the report, whether they are really there, and have arrived in Nuhashshe, and so I am sending Bethel to him. As soon as we meet with them, I will immediately send my messenger so he can report to you whether or not it is so.

To Rab-El,[5] Abdi-Eretz,[6] Turan,[7] and Adonizedek,[8] a message from Amur-Hadad.[9]

EA 170: To Aziru in Egypt

May all be well with you. Do not trouble yourselves, and do not worry at all. All is very well with your families here. Wish Anatu well.

EA 170 Notes

1 Cuneiform: Iškurlu Ia (𒀭𒅎𒇻𒅀)

Ishkur-lu Ia is often translated as Baaluya as Ishkur-lu as generally accepted as the Cuneiform spelling of 'Ba'al.' Ishkur was the Sumerian god of storms, the equivalent of the Akkadian storm-god Adad, whose Canaanite equivalent was Hadad. As Hadad was generally known as Ba'al (𐤁𐤏𐤋) in Canaanite which translates as 'Lord,' the term could refer to either the god Hadad or the term 'Lord.' The name Ia was not Sumerian, but is theorized by some to have been the Canaanite version of the Akkadian god Ea, which would imply the Canaanite god called Yam, which would make the name translate as 'Lord Yam.' It also appears to have been used during the Hyksos dynasty as the Amorite and Canaanite name for the constellation Taurus, based on the Egyptian word jḫ (𓇋𓎛𓃒), meaning 'ox,' which is believed to have been pronounced as jaḥa:waw during the era. The term continued to be used as a reference to a god until the end of the bronze age, appearing in Neshite (Hittite) and Alashiya (Cypriot) names, in addition to Phoenician names.

Tthe Israelitte book of 1st Paralipomenon (Παραλειπομένων Α') / Diḇrê Hayyāmîm (דברי־הימים) includes the name Baaliah (Βααλια / וּבְעַלְיָה), which appears to be a direct continuation of the name in the iron age, and so that name is used as a translation.

2 Cuneiform: Zuzilamaan (𒍪𒍣𒆷𒈠𒀭)

Zuzilamaan is believed to be a Hurrian name.

EA 170 Notes

3 Cuneiform: Amku (𒄠𒆪)

Amku is generally accepted as the ancient Egyptian name for the Beqaa Valley, in modern Lebanon. Some Egyptologists argue it was in Syria.

4 Cuneiform: Aaddumi (𒀀𒀜𒁺𒈪)

This name is considered to be the Cuneiform transliteration of the Egyptian name Åjtåmm (𓄿𓇋𓏏𓅓𓅓), a town also mentioned in the Israelite book of Joshua as Adummim (Αδδαμιν / אֲדֻמִּים), which is believed to have been somewhere between Jericho and Jerusalem, which would place it in the northern region of the modern Palestinian West Bank. So far, no archaeological site has been firmly identified with the site. The more common form of the name of Adummim, based on the Hebrew אדמים is used in this translation.

5 Cuneiform: Galan (𒃲𒀭)

Gal An translates as 'Great An,' 'Great God,' or 'Great Sky' in Akkadian. The Sumerian term Gal or Gala, was also the Akkadian term Kal, Qal, or Rab, while the 'dingir' referred to the sky-father god An, or the sky. In the Canaanite language, the dingir (𒀭) is accepted as referring to the god El, which results in the general translations for this name as Rab-El or Rab-Ilu. Equally valid translations are Kal-El, Kal-An, Qal-El, Qal-An, and Rab-An. The name may be the source of the term Galilee, which was Glyl (גליל) and Glyly (גלילי) in Hebrew and Aramaic.

EA 170 NOTES

6 Cuneiform: Ardu ^{an}Uraš (⟨cuneiform⟩)

Urash was the name of a Sumerian earth-mother goddess, and a consort of An (✳) the sky-father god. The ancient Canaanite equivalent of Urash, was Eretz, the earth-mother goddess. The logogram ardu (⟨cuneiform⟩) represented the term 'servant' or 'slave,' which was 'Abdi' in Canaanite, Aramaic, and Hebrew, resulting in the general translation of this name as Abdi-Urash. As the original name was Canaanite, the translation of Abdi-Eretz is used in this translation.

7 Cuneiform: Tur An (⟨cuneiform⟩)

The Sumerian logogram Dumu (⟨cuneiform⟩), which was pronounced as Tur in Akkadian, meant 'Son of,' 'Child of,' or 'Descendant of' in Sumerian and Akkadian, and therefore the name is often translated as Bin-Ana from Arabic or Ben-El from Hebrew. The Egyptian equivalent would have been Pen-Netjer, however, the name Turan is also documented in Mesopotamia, and therefore used in this translation.

8 Cuneiform: Gal Šidki (⟨cuneiform⟩)

The Sumerian term Gal or Gala, was also the Akkadian term Kal, Qal, or Rab, meaning 'great,' or 'prince.' The name Shidki (⟨cuneiform⟩) is likely an attempt to write Sydyk in Cuneiform, who was mentioned by Sanchuniathon as a Canaanite god circa 1200 BC. Sydyk was referred to in the Hebrew texts as Tzedek (צֶדֶק). This name appears to be a cuneiform spelling of Adonizedek (אֲדֹנִי־צֶדֶק) meaning 'lord

EA 170 NOTES

of justice,' found in the book of Hebrew Joshua, which is the translation used herein.

9 Cuneiform: Amur Iškur (𒀀𒈬𒌓)

• Translation: 'Ishkur has seen,' 'Adad has seen,' 'Hadad has seen,' 'Ba'al has seen'

As the Cuneiform text reads Iškur, not Iškurlu, the translation of Hadad is more probable than Ba'al, and therefore Amur-Hadad is used in this translation.

EA 189: Etakkama of Kadesh

Tell the king, my lord:

A message from Etakkama, your servant. I bow at the feet of my lord, my sun, seven times and another 7.

My lord, I am your servant, but the wicked Biryawaza has continually defamed me in your sight, my lord, and when he was defaming me in your sight, then he took my entire paternal estate along with the land of Kadesh,[1] and sent my cities up in flames. But, I assure you, the commissioners of the king, my lord, and his nobles know my loyalty, as I said to the magnate Pahura, "May the magnate Pahura know that [...damaged text...]."

[...damaged text...] Biryawaza. Therefore, I serve you, along with all my brothers, and wherever there is war against the king, I go, along with my soldiers and my chariots, and all my brothers. Since Biryawaza had allowed all of the cities of the king, my lord, to be captured by the Habirus from Tahash and Upu.[2] I went with your gods and your Sun leading me, and I restored from the Habirus, the cities to the king, my lord, for his service, and I disbanded the Habirus. May the king, my lord, celebrate Etakkama, his

EA 189: Etakkama of Kadesh

servant, as I serve the king, my lord, together with all my brothers. I serve the king, my lord, but Biryawaza caused the loss of all your lands. His intent is solely injustice, but I am your servant forever.

EA 189 Notes

1 Cuneiform: Kídšu (𒅗𒌑)

This is the Cuneiform spelling of Kadesh, the ancient city-state near the modern Syrian-Lebanese border.

2 Cuneiform: Upù (𒌑𒁉)

This is considered a reference to land near, or possibly surrounding Damascus.

EA 197: Biryawaza's plight

[...text damaged...] said to [...text damaged...] your servant was in A[...text damaged...] his horses and his chariots to the Habirus, and they did not give them to the king, my lord. Who am I? My purpose is to be your servant, and everything belongs to the king.

Biryawaza saw knew this and moved Yanuamma to rebellion against me. Having barred the city gate against me, he took chariots from Ashtara but gave both of them to the Habirus and did not give both of them to the king, my lord. When the king of Busruna and the king of Halunnu saw this, they allied with Biryawaza and waged war against me, saying, "Come, let's kill Biryawaza, and we will not let him go to [...text damaged...]

But, I got away from them and stayed in Damascus, but how can I serve the king, my lord? They keep saying, "We are servants of the Hittite king," and I keep replying, "I am a servant of the king of Egypt."

Arsawuya went to Kadesh, and took Aziru's troops, and captured Shaddu. He gave it to the Habirus and did not give it to the king, my lord. Now, since Etakkama has caused the loss of the

EA 197: Biryawaza's Plight

land of Kadesh, and since Arsawuya along with Biryawaza has caused the loss of Upu, may the king look carefully to his land or else the enemies take it. Since my brothers are at war with me, I am guarding Kamid al lawz, the city of the king, my lord.

May the king indeed be at one with his servant. May the king not abandon his servant, and ma] the kings of [...text damaged...] I have seen the archers.

EA 205: Ready for Marching Orders

Tell the king, my lord:

A message from the ruler of Tob,[1] your servant. I bow at the feet of the king, my lord, the sun of the people, seven times, and another seven times.

You have written to me to make preparations before the arrival of the archers. I am here, along with my infantry and my chariots, at the orders of the infantry of the king, my lord. Wherever they go.

EA 205 Notes

1 Cuneiform: Tubu (𒋫𒁄𒀀)

This is accepted as a reference to a town in southern modern Syria, referred to as Tob (טוֹב / Τωβ) in the Israelite book of Judges. The reference to Tob in the Book of Judges is from circa 1200 BC (Septuagint's chronology), around 150 years after the reference to Tubu in this letter, suggesting the city continued to exist until the end of the Bronze Age.

EA 223: Compliance With Orders

Tell the king, my lord, the sun in the sky:

A message from Endaruta, your servant. I bow myself to the feet of the king, my lord, seven times, and another seven times.

Whatsoever the king, my lord, orders, I will prepare.

EA 233: Work in Progress

Tell the king, my lord, the sun descended from the sky:

A message of Satatna the ruler of Acre, your servant, the servant of the king, and the dirt at his feet and the ground on which he treads, I bow at the feet of the king, my lord, my god, the sun from the sky, seven times and, another seven times, both on my stomach and on my back.

I am obeying what the king, my lord, has written to his servant, and preparing everything that my lord has commanded.

EA 234: An Order for Glass

Tell the king, my lord, the sun descended from the sky:

A message of Satatna, the ruler of Acre, your servant, the servant of the king, and the dirt at his feet, the ground on which he treads. I bow at the feet of the king, my lord, the sun from the sky, seven times and, another seven times, both on my stomach and my back.

May the king, my lord, listen to the word of his servant. Zirdamyaahda deserted Biryawaza. He was with Shuta a [...text damaged...] of the king, in the garrison city. He said nothing to him, and out came the troops of the king, my lord. He was with them in Megiddo. Nothing was said to him, and then he deserted to me, and Shuta has just written to me, "Hand over Zirdamyashda to Biryawaza."

I have not agreed to hand him over. Acre is like the fortifications[1] of Egypt. Has the king my lord, not heard that Shuta is turned against me? May the king, my lord, send his commissioner to take him away.

EA 234 Notes

1 Cuneiform: Magádalu (𒈠𒂵𒀠𒁺)

The word is Canaanite, and related to the Hebrew word mgdl (מגדל), which refers to a fortified tower of some kind. The Canaanite term is related to the Egyptian term môkảḏr (𓅓𓎡𓄜𓂋𓍘𓏤), which referred to a fortified place or fortified wall.

EA 235: An Order for Glass

Tell the king, my lord, my sun, my god, the sun descended from the sky:

A message of Satatna, your servant, the dirt at your feet. I bow at the feet of the king, my lord, my sun, my god, seven times and, another seven times.

I have obeyed the orders of the king's commissioner to me, to guard the cities for the king, my lord. I have guarded very carefully. Moreover, the king, my lord has written to me for glass, and I, therefore, send 50 sheets in weight, to the king, my lord.

EA 244: Labaya attacking Megiddo

Tell the king, my lord, and my sun:

A message of Biridiya, the loyal servant of the king. I bow at the feet of the king, my lord, and my sun, seven times and, another seven times.

May the king, my lord, know that since the return of the Egyptian archers, Labaya has attacked against me. We are thus unable to harvest, and we are unable to get out of the city gate, because of Labayu. When he learned that archers were not coming out, he immediately decided to take Megiddo. May the king save his city or else Labaya will seize it. Know that the city is consumed by pestilence, by [...text damaged...] Therefore, may the king give a garrison of 100 men, to guard his city or Labaya may seize it. Known that Labaya has no other intent. He simply seeks the seizure of Meggido.

EA 245: Assignment of Guilt

[...text damaged...]

Moreover, I urged my brothers, "If the god of the king, our lord, causes us to conquer Labaya, then we will quickly bring him alive to the king, our lord."

However, as my mare was shot, I followed behind him, and rode with Yashdata. But before my arrival, they had struck him down. Yashdata, being truly your servant, entered into battle alongside my. May [...text damaged...] the life of the king, my lord, that he may bring peace to everyone in the lands of the king, my lord.

It was Surata who captured Labaya from Megiddo. and told me, "I will send him to the king by boat."

Surata captured him, but he let him return home from Hannathon,[1] as Surata accepted a ransom from him. However, what have I done to the king, my lord, that he has treated me with contempt, and honored my less important brothers? It was Surata who let both Labaya and Ba'al-Mehr return to their homes.

May the king, my lord, know this.

EA 245 Note

1 Cuneiform: Ḫiinnatunu (𒄯𒉌𒋾𒉡)

The city of Hinnatunu is accepted as a reference to the of Hannathon / Ennathoth (חַנָּתֹן / Ενναθωθ) from the Hebrew Book of Joshua. Based on the dating found in the Septuagint, the reference is from around 1500 BC, when the city of Hannathon became part of the territory of the tribe of Zebulon.

EA 252: Sparing One's Enemies

Tell the king, my lord:

A message from Labaya, your servant. I bow at the feet of the king, my lord.

In regards to your having written to me, "Guard the men who seized the city," how am I to guard those men? The city was seized in war. When I had sworn my peace, and the officials swore along with me, the city, along with my god, was seized. He slandered me, and I am now slandered before the king, my lord.

Moreover, when an ant is struck [...damaged text...]

Moreover, when an ant is struck, does it not fight back and bite the hand of the man that struck it? How at this time can, I show deference when another city of mine will also be seized?

On the other hand, if you also order, "Fall down beneath them so they can strike you," I will do so. I will guard the men that seized the city and my god. They are the despoilers of my father, but I will guard them.

EA 254: Neither Rebel nor Delinquent

Tell the king, my lord, and my sun:

A message from Labaya, your servant, and the dirt on which you tread. I fall at the feet of the king, my lord, and my sun, seven times, and another seven times.

I have obeyed the orders that the king wrote to me. Who am I, that the king should lose his land on account of me?

It is a fact that I am a loyal servant of the king! I am not a rebel, and I am not delinquent in my duties. I have not held back my payments of tribute, and I have not held back anything requested by my commissioner. He denounces me unjustly, but the king, my lord, does not examine my act of rebellion.

Consider, my act of rebellion is this: When I entered Gezer,[1] I kept on saying, "Everything of mine the king takes, but where is that which belongs to Malik-El?"[2]

I know the actions of Malik-El against me! Moreover, the king wrote for my son. I did not know that my son was consorting with the

EA 254: Neither Rebel nor Delinquent

Habirus, and therefore I surrendered him to Addaya.[3] Nevertheless, if the king wrote to me, "Put a bronze dagger into your heart and die," how could I not follow the order of the king?

EA 254 Notes

1 Cuneiform: Gazru (𒁹𒂵𒍣)

The city of Gezer was a major fortified city-state, in southern Canaan (modern central Israel) along the road from Egypt to Syria. The remains of the city have been identified as Tel Gezer (גֶּזֶר), west of Jerusalem by multilingual inscriptions found at the site, dating to the 1st century BC.

According to the Israelite book of Joshua, the king of Gezer was killed by the armies of Joshua when they entered Canaan, circa 1508 BC (Septuagint's chronology), and the city subsequently fell under the jurisdiction of the Levitical Sons of Kohath priesthood. Archaeological evidence from the ruins of Tel Gezer shows the city was burnt down around 1500 BC, however, the destruction is generally attributed to Thutmose III's campaigns in southern Canaan in the 1450s BC, due to the older chronologies of Egyptology with placed the beginning of his reign circa 1500 BC. It is now accepted that he was born circa 1481 BC, and did not begin his campaigns in Canaan until after his aunt/step-mother/adopted-father Queen/King Hatsheput died, in approximately 1458 BC, and so he could not have been responsible for the destruction of Gezer.

After the destruction circa 1500 BC, the city was rebuilt, and became a major religious center in southern Canaan, as proven by the major massebot (large standing stones or menhirs) found at the site, and the double-cave below the massebot that was used for rituals. While there is no proof

EA 254 NOTES

that the priesthood at Gezer called themselves the Sons of Kohath, there is no evidence they did not either.

There are ten known letters from governors of Gezer to the house of Pharaoh among the Amarna Letters dating to the mid-1300s BC. During this era, a larger wall was built around the city, and a major palace was built in the western section of the city, along with what appears to be an Egyptian governor's residence. Archaeological evidence from the 1100s and 1000s BC, shows that the Canaanite population had declined and the Philistines appear to have become the dominant group. In the Israelite book of 1st Kingdoms (Masoretic Kings), the city was recaptured by the king of Egypt, before being transferred to King Solomon as a dowry, circa 950 BC.

2 Cuneiform: Milku An (𒈗𒀭)

- Translations: King God, King of the sky, King star

This name is accepted as an Akkadian transliteration of Malik-El, which could be translated as 'king El,' or 'Moloch is god.' A direct translation of the cuneiform could be read as King God, King of the sky, or King Star.

3 Cuneiform: Addaya (𒀀𒁕𒅀)

Addaya was an Egyptian official serving in southern Canaan during the era of Akhenaten. He is only mentioned in two of the known Amarna Letters, EA 254 from Labaya in Shechem and EA 287 from Abdi-Heba in Jerusalem.

EA 255: No destination too far

Tell the king, my lord, and my sun:

A message from Mut-Hadad,[1] your servant, the dirt at your feet, the muck you walk on. I bow at the feet of the king, my lord, seven times and, another seven times.

The king, my lord, sent Haaya to me saying, "A caravan to Mitanni,[2] is this sent on, so send it on!"

Who am I, that I would not send on a caravan of the king, my lord? Considering that Labaya, my father, served the king, his lord, and he himself used to send on all the caravans that the king sent to Mitanni. Let the king, my lord, send a caravan even to Babylon. I will personally convey it under very heavy guard.

EA 255 Notes

1 Cuneiform: Muútu Iškur (𒀀𒆪𒀭𒅎)

The name is generally interpreted as meaning Mut-Hadad, meaning 'man of Hadad.' Ishkur was the Sumerian storm-god, whose Akkadian equivalent was Adad, and whose Canaanite equivalent was Hadad Ba'al Hadad was the dominant god of the Amorite pantheon during the Middle Bronze age.

2 Cuneiform: Ḫanigalbad (𒄩𒉌𒃲𒁁)

Ḫanigalbad is accepted by Egyptologists as one of the names of the Mitanni Empire, based in the territory of modern Syria.

EA 256: Oaths and Denials

Tell yanhamu, my lord:

A message from Mut-Hadad, your servant. I bow at the feet of my lord.

How can it have been said in your presence, "Mut-Hadad has fled. He has hidden Job."[1]

How can the king of Pella[2] flee from the commissioner of the king, his lord?

The king and lord, he lives!

My king and lord, he lives!

My king and lord, be ashamed [...text damaged...]

As the king, my lord, lives!

As the king, my lord, lives!

I swear Job is not in Pella. In fact, he has been in the field for two months. Just ask Ben-Elima. Just ask Tadua. Just ask Joshua,[3] whether after he robbed Shulum-Marduk, I went to the aid of Ashtartu, when all the cities of the Golan Heights[4] had become hostile, and Edom,[5] Abarim,[6] Araru, Mesztu, Magdala, Kheni-anabi, and Sarqu.

EA 256: Oaths and Denials

Hayyanu, along with Yabiluma, has been captured.

Moreover, seeing that, after you sent me a tablet, I wrote to him, and before you arrive from your journey, he will surely have arrived in Pella. And I do obey your orders.

EA 256 Notes

1 Cuneiform: A'iaab (𒀀𒅀𒀊)

This name is generally transliterated as Ayyab. This is the same name as the Arabic Ayyub (أيوب) and Hebrew Iyyob (אִיּוֹב), the name of the prophet Job in the Quran and Masoretic texts. The Job in the Amarna Letters cannot be the Biblical/Quranic Job, as that Job would have lived around 2000 BC, based both on the astronomical alignments within both the texts of the Book of Job and the Testament of Job, as well as the lost Syriac book of Job's reference to Abraham being a close relative of Job. Nevertheless, the name Job (Ayyab, Ayyub, Iyyob) was a common Canaanite name by the 1300s BC, and therefore the common English name Job, derived from the Greek Iob (Ἰώβ) is used in this translation. This Job was likely the governor of the town of Ashtartu in southern modern Syria, mentioned in EA 364.

2 Cuneiform: Piḫili (𒉿𒄭𒇷)

This is accepted as the Akkadian spelling of the town of Pella, in northern-western modern Jordan.

3 Cuneiform: Iišuia (𒄿𒐊𒋗𒅀)

This is the Cuneiform spelling of the Aramaic name Yeshua (יֵשׁוּעַ), which later became the Hebrew Yehoshua (יְהוֹשֻׁעַ). The Aramaic Yeshua which was subsequently translated as Joshua in English, the name used in this translation. The Joshua in question has never been interpreted as the Biblical Joshua, as the chronology does not line up. In the Septuagint's Chronology, Joshua died

EA 256 Notes

around a century earlier, while in the Masoretic chronology, Joshua had not been born yet. As some scholars believe the Book of Joshua is a work of fiction, it is possible that the life of this Joshua is what the book was based on.

4 Cuneiform: Garu (𒄀𒊒)

This is accepted as a reference to the Golan Heights, in the modern Israeli-Syrian border region.

5 Cuneiform: Údumu (𒌑𒁺𒈬)

Údumu was the Cuneiform name of Edom, later called Idumaea by the Greeks and Romans. According to the Torah, the Edomites originally lived farther north, in northwest modern Jordan, and were pushed south into the region of modern southern Jordan and Israel by the Moabites, likely circa 1200 BC. This letter from the 1350s BC implies the same region, between the Golan Heights and Abarim.

6 Cuneiform: Aduru (𒀀𒁺)

This is accepted as the Cuneiform spelling of the name Abarim (הָעֲבָרִים), the mountain range in Jordan east of the Dead Sea.

EA 265: A gift acknowledge

Tell the king, my lord:

A message from Tagi[1], your servant.

I bow at the feet of the king, my lord.

My own man, I sent along with [...text damaged...] to see the face of the king, my lord.

The king, my lord, sent a present to me in the care of Tahmashshi, and Tahmashshi gave a gold goblet and 12 sets of linen garments.

For the information of the king, my lord.

EA 265 Notes

1 Cuneiform: Tagi (𒋫𒄀)

Tagi was the governor of the town of Gezer at Mount Carmel.

EA 269: Malik-El to the King

Tell my god, my king, my lord, my sun:

A message from Malik-El, your servant, the dirt at your feet. I fall at the feet of my god, my king, my lord, my sun, seven times and, another seven times.

I have heard what the king, my lord, wrote to me, and so may the king, my lord, send the archers to his servants, and may the king, my lord send myrrh for medication.

EA 270: Extortion

Tell the king, my lord, my god, my sun:

A message from Malik-El, your servant, the dirt at your feet. I bow at the feet of the king, my lord, my god, my sun, seven times, and another seven times.

May the king, my lord know the actions that Yanhamu keeps doing to me since I left the king, my lord. He wants 2000 shekels of silver from me, and he demands of me, "Surrender your wife and your sons, or I will kill you."

May the king know of these actions, and may the king, my lord, send chariots and return me to himself, or else I will die.

EA 271: The Power of the Habirus

Tell the king, my lord, my god, my sun:

A message from Malik-El, your servant, the dirt at your feet. I fall at the feet of the king, my lord, seven times, and another seven times.

May the king, my lord, know that the war against me, and against Shuwardata[1] is severe. So may the king, my lord, save his land from the power of the Habirus. Otherwise, may the king, my lord, send chariots to save us, or else our servants will kill us. Moreover, may the king, my lord, ask Yanhamu, his servant, about what is being done in his land.

EA 271 Notes

1 Cuneiform: Šuùaardata (𒋗𒄷𒅈𒁕𒋫)

Shuwardata is believed to have been the local governor of Gath / Gimti (𒂵𒅎𒋾) at the time. Gath was a city in southern Canaan during the New Kingdom era, which was re-settled by Sea Peoples as the New Kingdom disintegrated, becoming a Palestinian city in the early Iron Age.

EA 273: From a Queen-Mother

Tell the king, my lord, my god, my sun:

A message from the Lady of the Lions,[1] your handmaid. I bow at the feet of the king, my lord, seven times, and another seven times.

May the king, my lord, know that war has been waged in the land, and the land of the king has been lost, my lord, by desertion to the Habirus. May the king, my lord, take notice of his land, and may the king, my lord, know that the Habirus wrote to Ayalon[2] and Sarha,[3] and the two sons of Malik-El barely escaped being killed. May the king, my lord, know of these actions.

EA 273 Notes

1 Cuneiform: Nin Urmaḫmeš (𒁹𒊩𒌷𒈤)

The name is translated as 'Lady of the Lions' based on the of Babylonian 'Sumerograms' in the words, which translated directly as 'Lady Lions.' It is unclear if this was a name or a title. Multiple goddesses in the Middle East appear to have been the 'lady of the lions,' including the Sumerian Inanna, Akkadian (Babylonian, and Assyrian) Ishtar, Canaanite Astarte, and Egyptian Qetesh.

2 Cuneiform: Aiialuna (𒀀𒅀𒇻𒈾)

This is accepted as a reference to the Ayalon Valley in the Shephelah lowland in the Palestinian West Bank. The Ayalon Valley is one of the regions listed as occupied by the Hebrews in Joshua's invasion of Canaan in 1508 BC (Septuagint's chronology), which would suggest the Habirus mentioned in this letter were the Hebrews.

3 Cuneiform: Sarḫa (𒊬𒄩)

Sarha is a village in central Syria, in the Salamiyah District of Hama Governorate.

EA 274: Another city lost

Tell the king, my lord, my god, my sun:

A message from the Lady of the Lions, your handmaid, the dirt at your feet. I fall at the feet of the king, my lord, seven times, and another seven times.

May the king, my lord, save his land from the strength of the Habirus, or it will be lost. Sapuma has been captured. May the king, my lord, know of this.

EA 280: Another Labaya

Tell the king, my lord, my god, my sun:

A message of Shuwardata, your servant, the dirt at your feet. I bow at the feet of the king, my lord, my god, my sun, seven times and, another seven times.

The king, my lord, permitted me to wage war against Keilah, and I waged war. It is now at peace with me, and my city is restored to me. Why did Abdi-Heba write to the men of Keilah, "Accept silver and follow me?"

Moreover, Labaya, who used to take our towns, is dead, but now Abdi-Heba has become another Labaya, and he attacks our town. So, may the king consider his servant, because of this action...[...text damaged...]

EA 282: Alone

Tell the king, my lord, my god, and my sun:

A message from Shuwardata, your servant. I fall at the feet of the king, my lord, more than seven times, and another seven times, both when I arrive and I leave.

May the King, my lord, be aware that I am alone! Let the King, my lord, send me archers in great numbers and, save me! Let him rescue me!

May the King, my lord, know.

EA 283: Oh to see the king

Tell the king, my lord, my god, my sun:

A message from Shuwardata, your servant. I bow at the feet of the king, my lord. I bow at the feet of the king, my lord, seven times and 7 more times.

The king, my lord, has written to me, "Come and pay homage to me. Into the presence of the king, my lord!"

If only it were possible to enter the presence of the king, my lord, to receive the [...damaged text...] and the [...damaged text...] of the king, my lord. Since Yanhamu is with you, speak with him. If there are still no archers available, then may the king, my lord, take me away. May the king, my lord, be informed that 30 cities have waged war against me. I am alone! The war against me is terrible. The king, my lord, has thrown me from his hand. May the king, my lord, send archers.

May the king, my lord, take me away. Since Yanhamu, the commissioner of the king, my lord, is there, may the king, my lord, ask him, "Is the war against Shuwardata severe, or not?"

EA 286: A Throne Granted, Not Inherited

Tell the king, my lord:

A message from Abdi-Heba, your servant. I fall at the feet of my lord, the king, seven times, and seven times.

What have I done to the king, my lord, that they denounce me? I am slandered before the king, my lord, when they say, "Abdi-Heba has rebelled against the king, his lord."

Seeing that, as far as I am concerned, neither my father, nor my mother, put me in this place, but the strong arm of the king brought me into my father's house, why should I of all people commit a crime against the king, my lord?

As truly as the king, my lord, lives, I say to the commissioner of the king, "Lord, why do you love the Habirus but hate the mayors?" Therefore, I am slandered before the king, my lord.

Because I reported, "The lands of the king are lost, my lord," therefore, I am slandered before the king, my lord.

EA 286: A Throne Granted, Not Inherited

May the king, my lord, know that while the king, my lord, stationed a garrison here, Yanhamu has taken it all away.

My king, my lord, there is no garrison, so, may the king provide for his land. May the king provide for his land! All the lands of the king, my lord, have deserted.

Anammelech[1] has caused the loss of all the king's land, and so, may the king, my lord, provide for his land. For my part, I say, I would go down to the king, my lord, and visit the king, my lord, but the war against me is severe, and so I am not able to go down to the king, my lord.

May it seem good in the sight of the king, and may he send a garrison, so I may go down and visit the king, my lord.

In truth, as the king, my lord, lives, whenever the commissioners have come out, I reported, "The lands of the king are lost," but they did not listen to me. Lost are all the governors, there is not a governor remaining from the king, my lord.

May the king turn his attention to the archers, so that archers of the king, my lord, come out.

EA 286: A Throne Granted, Not Inherited

The king has no lands. The Habirus have plundered all the lands of the king. If there are archers this year, the lands of the king, my lord, will survive. But if there are no archers, the lands of the king, my lord are lost.

To the scribe of the king, my lord, a message from Abdi-Heba, your servant. Prepare eloquent words to the king, my lord. All the lands of the king, my lord are lost.

EA 286 Notes

1 Cuneiform: An Milku (✹𒈗)

• Translations: God King, sky King, star King, Anammelech

This name is composed of the cuneiform words An (✹) and Milku (𒈗), which appears to be the cuneiform translation of the name Anêmelech (Ανημελεχ) from the Septuagint's 4th Kingdoms, and Anammelech (עֲנַמֶּלֶךְ) in Masotetic Kings. As the name continued to be used in Canaan for more than 500 years, the more common Hebrew-derived pronouciation is used.

EA 287: A Very Serious Crime

Tell the king, my lord:

A message from Abdi-Heba, your servant. I bow at the feet of my lord seven times, and another seven times.

Consider the entire affair. Anammelech and Tagi brought troops into the town of Qiltu against me. Consider the actions they did against your servant. Arrows [...text damaged...] they brought into Qiltu. May the king know all the lands are at peace, however, I am at war. May the king provide for his land!

Consider the lands of Gezer, Ashkelon,[1] and Lachish.[2] They have given them food, oils, and any other requirement. Therefore, may the king provide archers, and send the archers against the men that commit crimes against the king, my lord.

If there are archers this year, then the lands and the governors will belong to the king, my lord. But if there are no archers, then the king will have neither lands nor governors.

Consider Jerusalem![3] This was given to me by neither my father nor my mother. The strong

EA 287: A Very Serious Crime

hand gave it to me. Consider the actions! These are the actions of Anammelech and the actions of the cohorts of Labaya, who have given the land of the king, to the Habirus.

Consider, my king, my lord! I am in the right! In regards the Kassites,[4] may the king inquire from the commissioners. Though the house is well fortified, they attempted a very serious crime. They took their tools, and I had to seek shelter under support of the roof. So if he is going to send troops into Jerusalem, let them come with a garrison for service. May the king provide for them, or all of the land might be in trouble because of their account.

May the king inquire about them. Let there be a great deal of food, oil, and clothing until Pauru, the commissioner of the king, comes up to Jerusalem. Addaya has left, together with the garrison of infantry the king provided. The king should know, Addaya said to me, "Know, he has dismissed me."

Do not abandon it, send a garrison this year, and send right here to the commissioner of the king! I sent gifts to the king, my lord, [...text damaged...]

EA 287: A Very Serious Crime

prisoners, 5000 [...text damaged...], 8 porters, for the caravans of the king, my lord, but they have been captured in the Ayalon Valley. May the king, my lord, know, I am unable to send a caravan to the king, my lord. For your information!

As the king has placed his name in Jerusalem forever, he cannot abandon the land of Jerusalem.

Tell the scribe of the king, my lord, a message from Abdi-Heba, your servant. I fall at your feet. I am your servant. Prepare eloquent words for the king, my lord. I am a soldier of the king. I am always yours.

Please state the Kassites are responsible for the evil actions. I was almost killed by the Kassites in my own house. May the king inquire in regards to them. May the king, my lord, provide for them. seven times, and more seven times, my the king, my lord, provide for me!

EA 287 Notes

1 Cuneiform: Aškaluna (𒀸𒅗𒇻𒈾)

This is the Cuneiform spelling of Ashkelon (אַשְׁקְלוֹן), a harbor city on modern Israel's Mediterranean coast. The city of Ashkelon was a major port-town in southern Canaan throughout the recorded history of the Canaan, mentioned in records of the New Kingdom as Jsqårnj (𓇌𓈎𓄿𓂋𓈖𓏭𓈉). Archaeological evidence indicates the town has existed since at least 5900 BC.

2 Cuneiform: Lakiši (𒆷𒆠𒅆)

This is accepted as the Cuneiform translation of Lachish (לכיש), an ancient town in modern Israel, between Jerusalem and Ashkelon. The city was a major town along the route from Egypt to Mesopotamia, and appears to have been the major trade-city in the Kingdom of Judah when the Assyrians and Egyptians plundered Judah in the 800s through 600s BC. In this line, the name is damaged in the middle, however, the entire name does survive in other places within the Amarna Letters, and the location is not in doubt in this letter.

3 Cuneiform: Urusalim (𒌑𒊒𒊓𒅴)

- Translation: City of Shalim, City of Dusk

This is accepted as the Cuneiform spelling of Jerusalem, the capital of modern Israel, and the historic Kingdoms of Judah and Judea.

EA 287 Notes

4 The Kassite Dynasty ruled Babylonia between circa 1595 and 1155 BC, and therefore, this reference can also be interpreted as the Old Babylonian Empire.

EA 288: Benign Neglect

Tell the king, my lord, my sun-god, my [...text damaged...]"

A message from Abdi-Heba, your servant [...text damaged...] I bow at the feet of my lord seven times, and another seven times.

Look, my king, my lord, you emplaced his name of Shalim,[1] and the rising-sun-god Shachar[2] who expands for me!

It is, impious what they have done to me. Know, I am not a governor. I am a soldier of the king, my lord. Know, I am a friend of the king and a tribute-carrier of the king. It was neither my father nor my mother, but the strong arm of the king that placed me in the house of my father. [...text damaged...] came to me [...text damaged...] I gave over to his charge 10 slaves.

Shuta, the commissioner of the king, came to me, and I gave over to Shuta's charge 21 girls, 80 prisoners, as a gift for the king, my lord. May the king consider his land, the land of the king has been lost. All of it has attacked me. I am at war as far as the land of Seir[3] and as far as Gezer at Carmel. All the governors are at peace, yet I am at

EA 288: BENIGN NEGLECT

war. I am treated like a Habiru, and I do not visit the king, my lord, since I am at war.

I am like a ship in the middle of the sea. The strong hand of the king captured the land of Syria,[4] and the land of Kush, but now the Habirus have taken the very cities of the king. Not a single governor remains loyal to the king, my lord, all are lost. Know that Turbazu was killed at the city gate of Shiloh,[5] and the king did nothing. Understand, servants who were allied to the Habirus killed Zimredda of Lachish, and Yaptih-Hadda was killed at the city gate of Siloh, yet the king did nothing.

Why has he not called them to account? May the king provide for his land and command that archers come out to his land. If there are no archers this year, all the lands of the king, my lord, are lost. They have not reported to the king that the lands of the king, my lord, are lost and all the governors are lost. If there are no archers this year, may the king send a commissioner to fetch me, me along with my brothers, and then we will die near the king, our lord.

To the scribe of the king, my lord:

EA 288: Benign Neglect

A message from Abdi-Heba, your servant. I bow at your feet.

Present the words that I have offered to the king, my lord, I am your servant and your son.

EA 288 Note

1 Cuneiform: mu si ᵃⁿUtu ši (𒈬𒋛𒀭𒌓𒅆)

- Translation: name of sliver (or finger) ᵍᵒᵈSun view (or sight)

The cuneiform translates as 'name of the setting sun-god.' The Canaanite god of dusk was Shalim, while the Egyptian dusk god was Atum. As the author, Abdi-Heba, was in Canaan, the Canaanite name is used in this translation.

2 Cuneiform: ᵃⁿUtu ši [...text damaged...] ḫaanpa (𒀭𒌓𒅆[...]𒄩𒀭𒉺)

- Translation: ᵈᵉⁱᵗʸSun view [...text damaged...] khaanpa

The text is damaged, however, does refer to a sun god, and uses what appears to be a transliteration of the Egyptian name Khepri (𓆣). Khepri was the Egyptian god of the dawn, whose Canaanite equivalent was Šḥr (𒄩𒊭𒄯) in the Ugaritc Texts from the same era. This name is generally translated as Shahar in English, influenced by the Hebrew word shachar (שַׁחַר), meaning dawn.

3 Cuneiform: Šeru (𒊺𒊒)

Sheru is considered the Cuneiform spelling of Seir, the ancient Edomite settlement in modern Jordan.

EA 288 NOTE

4 Cuneiform: Naaḫrima (𒈾𒀪𒄷𒊑𒈠)

Nahrima was the Egyptian name of western modern Syria, based on the Canaanite word 'Rivers.'

5 Cuneiform: Silu (𒍣𒇻)

Egyptologists have generally interpreted this as a reference to Tjaru (𓊽𓂋𓃭), as the Greeks later renamed it Selê (Σελη), which was continued into Coptic as Selê (Ⲥⲉⲗⲏ). The location of Tjaru is debated, but theorized to have been in the Sinai somewhere by Egyptologists, and the most often indicated location is the ruin at Tel el-Habua near Qantarah, northeast of the Nile. It is known that Tjaru was along the Road of Horus, which ran along the northern coastland of the Sinai peninsula, and then north to the Hurrian lands of modern Syria. While the Greeks may have built a fortress in the Sinai named Selê in Greek and Tjaru in Egyptian, this doesn't mean the original Tjaru was in the Sinai. It was recorded as being at the far reaches of Egypt during the New Kingdom, which at the time included Canaan and western Syria, suggesting it was in that region.

The town that Abdi-Heba was referring to, had to be near Jerusalem, as Abdi-Heba claimed he was cut off from Egypt by the governors he was fighting, which suggests that this was a reference to the fortified city of Shiloh north of Jerusalem. Shiloh had been a major fortified settlement from the Middle Bronze Age onward, and was along the road from Egypt to the Euphrates in Syria, yet, was not

EA 288 NOTE

mentioned in any Egyptian records, unless it was Tjaru / Silu.

The Israelite book of Judges claims that a King Jabin of Hazor occupied Samaria for a 20 year period between 1334 and 1314 BC (Spetuagint's dating), and that the Egyptians did not send any troops to restore order. The Samaritan city of Shiloh, was the holy city of the Israelites between approximately 1504 and 959 BC (Septuagint's dating). Jabin was ultimately killed by the Israelites after ruling for 20 years, and Egyptian rule was apparently restored five years into Pharoah Ay's rule. As this letter appears to date to the time of the rebellion, the translation of Shiloh is used for Silu.

EA 289: A Reckoning Demanded

Tell the king, my lord:

A message from Abdi-Heba, your servant. I bow at the feet of my lord, the king, seven times, and another seven times.

Malik-El does not leave from among the sons of Labaya, or from the sons of Arsawa, as they desire the land of the king for themselves. As for a governor who does this, why does the king not call him to account?

This was what Malik-El and Tagi did: they captured Arrabah.[1] Now as for Jerusalem, if this land belongs to the king, why isn't it of concern to the king, like Hazzatu? Gezer at Carmel[2] belongs to Tagi, and men of Gezer are the garrison in Beit She'an.[3] Are we to act like Labaya when he was giving the land of Shechem[4] to the Habirus?

Malik-El has written to Tagi and the sons of Labaya, "Both of you be a protection. Grant all their demands to the men of Keilah,[5] and let us isolate Jerusalem."

Addaya has taken the garrison that you sent to be under command of Haya, the son of Miyare, and he has stationed it in his own house in

EA 289: A Reckoning Demanded

Hazzatu and has sent 20 men to Egypt. May the king, my lord, know no garrison of the king is with me.

Accordingly, as truly as the king lives, his official Pu'uru, has left me and is in Hazzatu. May the king remember when me arrives. May the king send 50 men as a garrison to protect the land. The entire land of the king has been abandoned. Send Yanhamu so he may know about the land of the king, my lord.

To the scribe of the king, my lord, a message from Abdi-Heba, your servant.

Offer eloquent words to the king. I am always, utterly yours. I am your servant.

EA 289 Notes

1 Cuneiform: Rubutu (𒌷𒊏𒁍𒍣)

Rubutu is believed to have been a reference to the town of Arrabah, in the northern modern Palestinian West Bank.

2 Cuneiform: Ginti Kirimiil (𒄀𒅔𒋾 𒆠𒊑𒈪𒅋)

The name is believed to have referred to a town near Mount Carmel named Gezer. Another town was named Gezer farther south between Jerusalem and Ashkelon, however, the Gezer at Mount Carmel would have been in northern modern Israel.

3 Cuneiform: É Sanu (𒂍𒊓𒉡)

The É (𒂍) logogram, which means 'house' in Sumerian, was the cuneiform logogram used to represent the word 'beit,' also meaning house. This is believed to have been the Cuneiform spelling of Beit She'an, in northeast modern Israel. Archaeological evidence has proven that Beit She'an was a major Egyptian settlement in Canaan during the New Kingdom era. The town became a major Canaanite center between 1200 and 1000 BC. The Assyrians conquered Beit She'an with the rest of Samaria in 732 BC.

4 Cuneiform: Šakimu (𒊭𒆠𒈬)

Shakimu is accepted as a reference to Shemech (שְׁכֶם), the former town in the northern modern Palestinian West Bank, which is believed to have been located at the ruins of Tell Balata in the modern town of Nabulus. Shechem later

EA 289 Notes

became the capital of the first kingdom of Samaria in the 1260s BC (Septuagint's chronology).

5 Cuneiform: Kiiltu (𒆥𒅋𒌅)

This is accepted as a reference to the former town of Keilah (קעילה / قيلة), in the southern modern Palestinian West Bank, at the ruins of Kh. Qeila.

EA 290: Three Against One

Tell the king, my lord:

A message from Abdi-Heba, your servant. I bow at the feet of the king, my lord, seven times and, another seven times.

Here are the actions against the land that Malik-El and Shuwardata did against the land of the king, my lord. They commanded troops from Gezer, troops from Gath, and troops from Keilah. They seized Arrabah. The lands of the king have been abandoned to the Hapirus.

Besides this, a town belonging to Jerusalem, named Bethlehem,[1] a city of the king, has gone over to the side of the men of Keilah. May the king pay attention to Abdi-Heba, your servant, and send archers to restore the land of the king to the king. If there are no archers, the land of the king will desert to the Hapirus. This action against the land was at the order of Malik-El and at the order of Shuwardata, along with Ginti. May the king provide for his land!

EA 290 Notes

1 Cuneiform: É ᵃⁿNinurta (𒂍𒀭𒊹)

The É (𒂍) was the Akkadian logogram meaning 'house,' used to represent the Canaanite word 'beit,' also meaning 'house.' Ninurta was the Akkadian agricultural and warrior god, and the equivalent of the Canaanite fertility agricultural and warrior god Lehem. Therefore, this is most likely a reference to the Canaanite town of Bethlehem, south of Jerusalem.

EA 299: A Plea for Help

Tell the king, my lord, my god, the sun, the sun descended from the sky:

A message from Yapahu, the ruler of Gezer, your servant, the dirt at your feet, the groom of your horses. Honestly, I bow at the feet of the king, my lord, my god, my sun, the sun from the sky, seven times and, another seven times, on my stomach and on my back.

I have listened to the words of the messenger of the king, my lord, very carefully. May the king, my lord, the sun descended from the sky, consider this land. Since the Habirus are stronger than we, my the king, my lord, give me his help, and may the king, my lord, save me from the Habirus or else the Habirus may destroy us.

EA 303: Careful Listening

Tell the king, my lord, my god, my sun, the sun descended from the sky:

A message from Shubandu, your servant, and the dirt at your feet, the groom of your horses. I bow myself, on my stomach and on my back, at the feet of the king, my lord, the sun descended from the sky, seven times and, another seven times.

I have heard all the words of the king, my lord, the sun from the sky, and I am indeed guarding the land of the king where I am. I have listened to Tahmashshi very carefully.

EA 314: A shipment of glass

Tell the king, my lord, my god, my sun descended from the sky:

A message from Pu-Ba'al,[1] your servant, the ruler of Yursa. I bow myself at the feet of the king, my lord, my god, my sun, the sun descended from the sky, seven times and, another seven times, on my back and on my stomach.

I am guarding the land of the king, my lord, my sun, the sun descended from the sky. Who is the dog that would not obey the orders of the king, the sun descended from the sky? Since the king, my lord, has ordered some glass, I send it to the king, my lord, my god, the sun descended from the sky.

EA 314 Note

1 Cuneiform: Pù Balu (𒅴𒁀𒇻)

This is considered a transliteration of the Canaanite words meaning Voice of Ba'al, or Herald of Ba'al.

EA 316: Postscript to the royal scribe

Tell the king, my lord, my god, my sun descended from the sky:

A message from Pu-Ba'al, your servant, and the dirt at your feet, the groom of your horses. I bow at the feet of the king, my lord, my god, my sun descended from the sky, seven times and, another seven times, on my back and on my stomach.

I am guarding the land of the king carefully. Who is the dog that would neglect the command of the king? I am obeying the orders of Tahmashshi, the commissioner of the king.

Tell the scribe of my lord, a Message of Pu-Ba'al. I bow at your feet. There was nothing in my house when I entered it, and so I have not sent a caravan to you. I am now preparing a fine caravan for you.

EA 321: Listening carefully

Tell the king, my lord, my god, my sun, the sun descended from the sky:

A message from Judah,[1] the governor of Ashkelon, your servant, the dirt at your feet, the groom of your horses. I bow myself on my stomach and on my back, before the feet of the king, my lord, the sun descended from the sky seven times, and again seven times.

Regarding the commissioner of the king, my lord, whom the king my lord, the sun descended from the sky, sent to me, I have listened to his orders very carefully. I am vigilantly guarding the land of the king where I am.

EA 321 Notes

1 Cuneiform: IIDIIA (𒂊𒅀𒁕𒀀)

This appears to be an early Canaanite spelling of the name Judah, and is virtually identical to the Canaanite pronunciation of the name YHDH (𐤄𐤃𐤄𐤉) from a few centuries later, and similar to the Neo-Assyrian Cuneiform spelling was IAUDAAA (𒅀𒌑𒁕𒀀𒀀) around 700 years later.

EA 323: A Royal Order for Glass

Tell the king, my lord, my god, my sun, the sun descended from the sky:

A message from Judah, your servant, the dirt at your feet, the groom of your cavalry. I bow prostrate myself, on my back and on my stomach, at the feet of the king, my lord, seven times and, another seven times.

I am vigilantly guarding the land of the king, my lord, and the city of the king, following the command of the king, my lord, the sun from the sky. Regarding the king, my lord, having ordered some glass, I send with this message 30 sheets of glass to the king, my lord. Who is the dog that would not obey the orders of the king, my lord, the sun descended from the sky, the son of the sun, whom the sun loves?

EA 325: Preparations Completed

Tell the king, my lord, my god, my sun, the sun descended from the sky:

A message from Judah, your servant, the dirt at your feet, the groom of your horses. I bow myself on my back and on my stomach, at the feet of the king, my lord, seven times and, another seven times.

I am guarding the land of the king, my lord, and the city of the king, my lord, where I am. Who is the dog that would not obey the orders of the king, the sun descended from the sky? I have prepared absolutely everything: food, alcohol, oxen, sheep, goats, grain, straw, and absolutely everything that the king, my lord, commanded. I have prepared it. I am also preparing the tribute to the sun, following the command of the king, my lord, the sun from the sky.

EA 325: Preparations under way

Tell the king, my lord, my god, my sun, the sun descended from the sky:

A message from Zimreddi, the ruler of Lachish, your servant, the dirt at your feet. I bow at the feet of the king, my lord, the sun from the sky, seven times and, another seven times.

In regards to the messenger that the king, my lord, sent to me, I have listened to his orders very carefully, and I am making preparations as per his orders.

EA 337: Governor of the City

Tell the king, my lord, my sun, my god:

A message from Hiziru, your servant. I bow at the feet of the king, my lord, seven times and, another seven times.

The king, my lord, wrote to me, "Prepare the supplies before the arrival of a large army of archers from the king, my lord." May my god, the king, my lord, permit the king, my lord, come out along with his large army and learn about his lands. I have prepared abundant supplies before the arrival of a large army of the king, my lord.

The king, my lord, wrote to me, "Guard Maya," the commissioner of the king, my lord. Honestly. I am guarding Maya very carefully.

EA 362: A Commissioner Murdered

From Rib-Haddi:

Tell the king, my lord. I bow at the feet of my lord seven times and, another seven times.

I have heard the words of the king, my lord, and I celebrated. May my lord quickly send archers as fast as possible. If the king, my lord, does not send archers, then we ourselves will die and Byblos will be captured. It was in danger recently, and it is also in danger now. Recently they were saying, "There will be no archers," but I wrote, and the result was that archers came out and captured their fatherland.

Now again they are saying, "Let him not write, or we will certainly be captured."

They seek to capture Byblos, and they say, "If we capture Byblos, we will be strong, and there will not be a man left, they will certainly be too few."

I, for my part, have guarded Byblos, the king's city, day and night. If I move to the hinterlands, then the men will desert in order to take territory for themselves, and there will be no men to guard Byblos, the city of the king, my lord.

EA 362: A Commissioner Murdered

Therefore, may my lord rush the archers, or we will die. My lord has written to me that they know that they are going to die, and so they seek to commit a crime. As to his having said before the king, "There is a plague in the lands," the king, my lord, should not listen to the words of other men. There is no plague in the lands. It has been over for a long time. My lord knows that I do not write lies to my lord. All the governors are not in favor of the archers' coming out, for they have peace. I am the one who wants them to come out, for I have trouble.

May the king, my lord, come out, for I have trouble. Look, the day you come out, all the lands will be rejoined the king, my lord. Who will resist the infantry of the king?

May the king, my lord, not leave this year free for the sons of Abdi-Asherah, for you know all their hateful acts against the lands of the king. Who are they that they have committed a crime and killed the commissioner Pawura?

EA 363: A joint report on the Beqaa Valley

Tell the king, my lord, my god, my sun:

A message from Abdi-Risha,[1] your servant, the ruler of Enishasi.[2] I bow in the dirt before the feet of the king, my lord, seven times and again seven times.

Look, we are in the Beqaa Valley, and the cities of the king, my lord. Etakkama, the ruler of Kadesh,[3] assisted by soldiers from Hatti,[4] set to fire the cities of the king, my lord. May the king, my lord, consider it, and may the king, my lord, send archers that we may regain the cities of the king, my lord, and dwell in the cities of the king, my lord, my god, my sun.

EA 363 Notes

1 Cuneiform: Arduriša (𒀵𒊑𒅖𒄿𒊭)

Abdi-Risha was the governor of the city-state of Enishasi in the Beqaa Valley in the mid-1300s BC.

2 Cuneiform: Enišasi (𒌷𒂊𒉌𒊭𒋛)

Enishasi was a city-state in the Beqaa Valley of modern Lebanon, in the mid-1300s BC. Enishasi was located southwest of Baalbek in Lebanon.

3 Cuneiform: Kinšu (𒆧𒋗)

This is accepted as a translation of Kadesh, the ancient city-state near the modern Syrian-Lebanese border. Kadesh was also transliterated as Kidšu (𒆠𒋗) in other letters, and the spelling in this letter may be an error.

4 Cuneiform: Ḫatti (𒄩𒀜𒋾)

Khatti was the Neshite (Hittite) capital.

EA 364: Justified War

Tell the king, my lord:

A message from Job, your servant. I bow at the feet of my lord seven times, and another seven times. I am the servant of the king, my lord, and the dust under his two feet.

I have obeyed the message from the king, my lord, delivered to me by the hand of Atahmaya. I will continue diligently guard the lands of the king, my lord. However, known that the king of Hazor[1] has captured 3 towns from me! On the day that I heard, I ordered to begin hostilities against them until the king, my lord, may be notified, and the king, my lord, may make a decision concerning his land.

EA 364 Notes

1 Cuneiform: Ḫasura (𒄩𒋩𒊏)

This is accepted as the Cuneiform spelling of Hazor was a city located at Tel Hazor (תל חצור), in northeast modern Israel. Based on the time period, this king of Hazor would be Jabin of Hazor, whose rebellion against Egypt was recorded in the Israelite book of Judges. This correlation depends of using the dating found in the Septuagint, not the Masoretic text.

EA 365: Furnishing Forced Laborers

Tell the king, my lord, my sun:

A message from Biridiya, your faithful servant of the king. I bow at the feet of the king, my lord, and my sun, seven times and another seven times.

May the king, my lord, know about his servant and his city. Know that I alone am farming around the town of Shunem,[1] and I provide the forced labor. Know that the governors near me are not doing what I do. They do not farm near the town of Shunem, and they do not provide forced labor. I am the only one providing forced laborers, from the town of Jaffa,[2] from my own resources, as well as from the town of Nuribta. Now, may the king, my lord know about his city.

EA 365 Notes

1 Cuneiform: Šunama (𒋗𒈾𒈠)

The name is considered the Cuneiform the spelling of Shunem (Σουνὰν / שׁוּנֵם), a small town in the Jezreel Valley mentioned in the Egyptian records of the Canaanite conquests of Thutmose III and Shoshenk I, and Hebrew Books of Joshua, 1st Kingdoms (Samuel), and 3rd Kingdoms (Kings). In transliterated ancient Egyptian, the name was Šnåmmå (𓈖𓂝𓅓) during the era.

2 Cuneiform: Iapù (𒅀𒉿)

This is believed to have been a reference to Jaffa, on the Mediterranean coast of modern Israel.

EA 366: A rescue operation

Tell the king, my lord, my sun, my god:

A message from Shuwardata, your servant, the servant of the king and the dirt at your feet, and the ground you tread on. I bow at the feet of the king, my lord, the sun in the sky, seven times and, another seven times, both on my stomach and on my back.

May the king, my lord, be informed that the Habirus that rebelled against the lands of the god of the king, my lord, were captured by me, and I killed him. May the king, my lord, be informed that all my brothers have abandoned me. Only Abdi-Heba and I have been at war against the Habirus. Surata, the governor of Acre, and Endaruta, the governor of Achshaph,[1] have also come to my assistance with 50 chariots, and now they are on my side in the war. May it seem right in the sight of the king, my lord, and may he send Yanhamu, so that we may all wage war and you restore the land of the king, my lord, to its frontiers.

EA 366 Notes

1 Cuneiform: Agšapa (𒀝𒊭𒉺)

This city was mentioned in numerous texts from the Egyptian New Kingdom era, through the early Kingdoms of Israel era. The city's name translates as 'sorcery' in Canaanite, and was known as Jksp (𓇋𓎡𓊃𓊪) in Egyptian. It was later translated as Axiph (Ἀξείφ) in Greek, and Achshaf (אַכְשָׁף) in Hebrew. The location was described as being at the eastern edge of the tribe of Asher's territory in the Book of Joshua, which would place it inland, somewhere in northern Israel, or southern Lebanon, today.

EA 367: From the Pharaoh to Endaruta

Tell Endaruta, the governor of Achshaph:

A message from the king.

This tablet I have sent to you, to tell you to stand guard! Be on guard over the land of the king, that is assigned to you. The king has sent to you, Hani son of Maireya, the Chief of Cavalry of the king in Canaan, and you will listen very carefully to what he tells you, unless the king finds in you an evil action. Every word that he says to you, obey it very carefully, and carry it out exactly. Stand guard! Guard, and do not be weak. Make sure that you prepare plenty of food, plenty of wine, and everything else, for the king's archers and infantry. He will reach you very, very quickly, and he will cut off the heads of the enemies of the king. Be informed that the king is hale like the sun in the sky, and his infantry and his chariotry are very, very well as well!

EA 368: A consignment of personnel

Tell the king, my lord, my god, my sun:

A message from Malik-El, your servant, the dirt at your feet. I fall at the feet of the king, my lord, my god, my sun, seven times and, another seven times.

May the king, my lord, know that the city of the king, my lord, that he put under my command, is safe and sound, and the word [...text damaged...] I send in the care of Haya, 46 female [...text damaged...] and 5 male [...text damaged...] and 5 ashiruma[1] to the king, my lord.

EA 368 Notes

1 Cuneiform: Aširuma (𒐁𒅗𒊺𒊒𒈠)

This term is not clearly understood, as the majority of the sentence is damaged. It may be a Canaanite plural form of the Egyptian word åšr (𓄿𓇋𓊃𓂋), meaning 'roast,' or 'sacred offering.'

EA 369: From the Pharaoh to Malik-El

Tell Malik-El, the ruler of Gezer:

A message from the king.

He dispatches this tablet to you, tell you, with it he sends to you Hanya, the commander of the archers, along with everything required for the acquisition of beautiful female cupbearers: silver, gold, linen garments, carnelian, and all sorts of gems, an ebony chair, all equally fine things. Total: 160 diban. Total: 40 female cupbearers, 40 silvers being the price of a female cupbearer.

Send extremely beautiful female cupbearers in whom there is no defect, so the king, your lord, will say to you, "this is excellent, as he ordered to you." Know that the king is well, like the sun. His troops, his chariots, his horses, all are very well. Amen has put the Upper Land and the Lower Land, where the sun rises, and where the sun sets, under the feet of the king.

EA 370: Preparations completed

Tell the king, my lord, my god, my sun, the sun descended from the sky:

A message from Judah, your servant, the dirt at your feet, the groom of your horses. I bow myself, on my back and on my stomach, at the feet of the king, my lord, seven times and, another seven times

I am guarding the land of the king, my lord, and the city of the king, my lord, where I am. Who is the dog that would not obey the orders of the king, the sun from the sky? I have prepared absolutely everything: food, alcohol, oxen, sheep, goats, straw, and absolutely everything that the king, my lord, commanded. I have prepared it. I am preparing the tribute of the sun, following the command of the king, my lord, the sun descended from the sky.

Also Available in Print

SEPTUAGINT SERIES:
- Septuagint: Cosmic Genesis
- Septuagint: Exodus
- Septuagint: Leviticus
- Septuagint: Numbers
- Septuagint: Deuteronomy
- Septuagint: Joshua
- Septuagint: Judges and Ruth
- Septuagint: Kingdoms
- Septuagint: Paralipomena
- Septuagint: Ezra
- Septuagint: Tobit
- Septuagint: Judith
- Septuagint: Esther
- Septuagint: Maccabees
- Septuagint: Psalms and the Prayer of Manasseh
- Septuagint: Job
- Septuagint: Solomon
- Septuagint: Wisdom of Joshua ben Sira and Odes
- Septuagint: Torah
- Septuagint: History, Volume 1

ALSO AVAILABLE IN PRINT

- Septuagint: History, Volume 2
- Octateuch: The Original Orit
- Dodeka: Book of Prophets

ENOCH AND METATRON SERIES:
- Books of Enoch Collection
- Books of Enoch and Metatron Collection
- Books of Metatron Collection
- Secrets of Enoch

OTHER TRANSLATIONS:
- Life of Adam and Eve
- Septuagint's Esther and the Vetus Latina Esther
- Septuagint's Ezekiel and the Ba'al Cycle
- Septuagint's Job and the Testament of Job
- Septuagint's Proverbs and the Wisdom of Amenemope
- Septuagint's Solomon and the Testament of Solomon
- The Amarna Letters
- Testaments of the Patriarchs Collection
- Tobit and Ahikar
- Ugaritic Texts: Ba'al Cycle
- Wisdom of Ahikar

www.ingramcontent.com/pod-product-compliance
Lightning Source LLC
Chambersburg PA
CBHW071343080526
44587CB00017B/2943